East Belfast

From Harbour to Hills

Paintings by Martin D. Cooke
Text by Keith Haines

Cottage Publications

First published by Cottage Publications,
Donaghadee, N. Ireland 2001.
Copyrights Reserved.
© Illustrations by Martin D. Cooke 2001.
© Text by Keith Haines 2001.
Design & origination in Northern Ireland.
Printed & bound in Singapore.

ISBN 1 900935 23 6

The Author

Keith Haines has recently retired from teaching, having been Head of History at Campbell College for over 20 years.

He is the compiler of *Images of Ireland: East Belfast* and *North Down Memories*, and has written the history of Campbell College as well as numerous articles, primarily on local history.

Keith has been secretary of the East Belfast Historical Society for ten years, and is the current editor of its Journal. He also created the Society website. He is a member of the Management Committee of the Federation for Ulster Local Studies, and edits its magazine, *Due North*.

Keith's primary interest is researching the lives of unknown local characters and has travelled to the Balkans, Albania and Iran on the trail of one of then - Arthur Moore.

The Artist

Martin D. Cooke UWS was born and educated in Belfast. After leaving school he spent five years as an architectural draughtsman followed by a further four years in a successful restaurant business, thus combining his passions for painting and cooking.

In 1978, the success of his first one-man exhibition prompted him to turn professional. He has hosted numerous exhibitions since throughout Ireland as well as America.

He draws his inspiration from the Irish countryside as well as the Lake District, a favourite walking location.

Martin is a member of the Ulster Watercolour Society and his work has attracted the attention of numerous collectors at home and abroad.

Contents

Noble Barons or Robber Barons?

Glancing at the multiplicity of roads, countless domestic terraces, essential commercial buildings, punctuating shops, churches, schools and relentless industrial heritage, it requires a stretch of the imagination to accept that half a millennium - and even half that time - ago the whole of East Belfast was entirely green, rural and, probably, unspoiled. As Rev John Redmond, the vicar of St Patrick's Ballymacarrett (1920-29), pointed out, the latter townland - which is only one part of the wider district of East Belfast - was, by the start of the 20th century, as populous as many Irish towns and cities, such as Limerick, Armagh and Lisburn. Man's foothold had become permanent, and the rural aspect had long since started to fade in the memory.

The O'Neills of Clandeboye

In the 15th century the influence of the O'Neill family gathered momentum under Hugh the Yellow (or Hugh Boy). His estates - referred to in Irish as *Clann Aodhe Buidhe* - are recorded in a map of 1591 as Claneboy. Eventually this nomenclature, like all things Irish, was Anglicised to Clandeboye. The O'Neill territories were divided into Lower Clandeboye, which incorporated Belfast (to the north of the Lagan) and the Co Antrim estates, and southern or Upper Clandeboye which encompassed North Down and the Ards.

Castlereagh, the chief residence of this latter branch of the family - which probably stood on the site of the former Orange Hall (now Belmont Carpets) on the brow of Church Road - was perhaps first built in the late 14th century in what became the parish of Knockbreda, in Castlereagh in the hills overlooking Belfast. Its name is derived from the Irish *an caisleán riabhach* - the grey castle - and was, in 1552, described as standing "on the plain in the midst of the woods of Dufferin". In 1744, it was located by Walter Harris:

"Not much more than two miles east of Belvoir, and about as much south-east of [the Long] Bridge, are the ruins of an ancient castle, called Castlereagh, from whence the Barony of that name is denominated. It is situated on top of a hill ... the fort has a fosse which encompasses three-quarters of it ... In the midst of the fort stood a castle, formerly the seat of Con O'Neill, proprietor

of that large tract of country [224 townlands in all], *which was afterwards divided among Lords Clandeboye, Ards and the ancestors of the present Lord Hillsborough".*

The most pessimistic interpretation would state that history is a succession of examples of individuals - kings, local chieftains, ambitious generals, petty tyrants, voracious landowners - seeking to maximise their power and wealth. For most people, it has been irrelevant who their lord or landlord was; the vast majority of people have been exploited by the most ruthless opportunist of the age.

The history of the British Isles abounds with examples of such predatory actions. One suspects that elevation to early Anglo-Saxon kingship owed most to the ability of an individual to raise the largest band of thugs to intimidate the neighbourhood. In 1066, if Harold Godwinesson of England or Harald Hardrada of Norway had prevailed instead of William of Normandy, they would have found justifiable reasons to consign their rivals to the status of wrongful ambition. Success and survival have depended more upon ruthlessness, instinct and the fortunes of war than upon right and justice.

Co Down was similarly afflicted in the late 16th and early 17th centuries, when English and Scottish adventurers eyed the tempting territories of the local Irish chieftains, the O'Neills. In the 1570s Sir Thomas Smith and the Earl of Essex were granted the lands of the O'Neills - despite the fact that the queen had recently confirmed them to the native family - and, when English expeditions landed at Strangford, the O'Neills rampaged through North Down causing great destruction.

At this time the chieftain of Upper Clandeboye was Niall MacBrian Ertaugh, the son of Brian Fagartach O'Neill, who had been killed in 1548. It was muttered by some that this branch of the family had themselves stolen possession of Upper Clandeboye in troubled times, but there was connivance at their occupation for the sake of peace. The Earl of Essex had made Niall Captain of Clandeboye, in return for which title Niall was expected to levy forty horseman and eighty infantry for Her Majesty.

Con O'Neill

Niall's son, Con, succeeded his father in 1600 or the following year, and became a royalist, benefiting from the royal purse in the midst of the Nine Years' War (1594-1603) between the Crown and the Irish earls. Con - whose full name was Con McNiall McFagartach O'Neill - suffered the indignity of briefly losing Castlereagh to Bryan MacArt O'Neill, a very distant relation, but it was recaptured and returned to him by Sir Arthur Chichester in July 1601. About three years later some of the extensive Clandeboye estates were depicted as "depopulated and wasted", but Con was distracted by his own problems. He has been described as "a singularly unfortunate and incapable native chief", and by the time of his death in c.1619 he had lost control of much of his property - originally said to have been worth around £12,000 per annum - including that in what is now East Belfast.

Con's downfall was very much the product of his own devising and human weakness. There must have been a time when young Con exhibited much promise, as he was elected local chieftain (or *Teirne*) by his peers according to the Irish law of tanistry. However, about a year after his restoration to his own castle he had found accommodation in another - the sturdier edifice at Carrickfergus - charged with levying war and treason against the queen. Her Virgin Majesty was to pass away on 24 March 1603 but, far from ameliorating his predicament, the accession of the Scot, King James I, was only to accelerate Con's problems.

The capital charge against the Clandeboye chieftain had come about as the result of a fairly trivial incident. Con was engaged in drunken revelry at Castlereagh with his family, friends and followers. He despatched some of his men, who were probably already the worse for drink, into Belfast to replenish his wine cellar. As tends to happen on these occasions, a fight ensued with some English soldiers, and his men returned to the hills battered and, perhaps more to Con's chagrin, without the wine! They were browbeaten and embarrassed into returning to Belfast, but a further fight broke out, and a number of men were killed. Beaten and pursued, Con's men retreated again, but the soldiers considered it imprudent to venture into the Castlereagh foothills. Con was arrested and charged shortly afterwards.

Con's treatment in Carrickfergus was relaxed, but he remained a prisoner after Elizabeth's death. His predicament provided an opportunity for the astute, ambitious Scot, Hugh Montgomery, sixth laird of Braidstane. One of the latter's relatives seduced the daughter of the marshal at the Norman castle and, using ropes smuggled in by his wife in hollowed-out cheeses, Con was able to escape across the Irish Sea.

Montgomery promised that he could obtain O'Neill's pardon and release at court. This, inevitably, was at a price - half of Con's estates! In no position to argue, Con agreed, but before the original patents could be ratified, others at court suggested that Upper Clandeboye was too extensive for two men, and Con and Montgomery had to divide it further with James Hamilton!

The arrangement between the three men proved

complex, but on 6 November 1605, James Hamilton confirmed Con in sixty-eight of his former townlands, of which many were in present-day East Belfast. These included Breda, Braniel, Ballyrushboy (now across the Castlereagh Road), Galwally, Cregagh, in addition to Ballymacarrett and Castlereagh.

Whether, during his final years, Con was demoralised or simply incompetent will never be known, but he proved unable to adapt to the new world order, and the shrewd, voracious adventurers probably found it easy to manipulate him. Although Con enjoyed all the rights and privileges of a landlord, he was prevented from claiming his rents in the traditional Irish fashion. He started to sell his land; the impoverished chieftain left his home on the hill overlooking Belfast, and by 1613 may have been living at Ballyhanwood (near Dundonald). He died circa 1619, and is possibly buried in south Holywood.

There is a considerable irony in the fact that Con's elder son Domhnall (or Donal) - known to the English as Daniel - grew up amongst ineptitude and chicanery in the Castlereagh Hills to become an able and respected figure at the court of King Charles II. Although he failed on two occasions to recover his father's estates, this ruddy-faced Ulsterman, of medium build, sporting light brown hair and almost clean-shaven, remained loyal to the Crown during the years of Civil War in the 1640s, even

managing to be one of the few ever to escape from the Tower of London.

Daniel married a countess, became an MP, and served Charles II in positions of responsibility. How envious Daniel's father would have been to know that his son became the sole manufacturer of gunpowder to the Crown and - closer to home - accountant for the regulation of ale-houses! Con's inability to hang on to his wealth was in stark contrast to his son's elevation in 1662 to the rank of postmaster-general, from which office he probably made well over £25,000 per annum; yet, following his death in 1664, he was described by the king as being "as honest a man who ever lived".

The abandoned O'Neill castle in Castlereagh fell to ruin, and is likely to have been used as a quarry for stone - just as stone from the Marquis of Donegall's Ormeau House was used to build Robb's warehouse in Castle Place. In or around 1809, according to one commentator, the castle "met with a truly Irish fate". The tenant occupying that area was requested by the Marquis of Downshire,

"to build a wall around the ruins with the laudable intention of preserving them from further dilapidation. The tenant, indeed, built a good and substantial wall,

but unluckily he employed the materials of the old castle itself for the purpose"!

The wall was still there to be seen by Dr Alexander Knox in 1875, and was sketched by the celebrated East Belfast artist J W Carey as he roamed the Castlereagh Hills twenty years later.

Later Owners of East Belfast

Sir Moses Hill, whose family became the Marquises of Downshire, bought from Con the manor of Castlereagh and eight townlands which included Braniel, Cregagh, Ballymaconaghy (effectively the top of the Cregagh Road area) and Ballynafeigh, which represented the beginnings of over 100,000 acres of family estate in Co Down. Con also conveyed land in Ballymacarrett in 1609 to a Scottish planter named Colonel David Boyd, and then to James Cathcart, before it fell under the control of James Hamilton, Viscount Clandeboye.

The majority of Con's original estate was divided between the latter and Sir Hugh Montgomery, and their disputed, ill-defined boundaries led to litigation which was to drag on for over thirty years and cost £1400. The hard-nosed Viscount determined to justify his claims, and in 1625 hired Thomas Raven who commenced his historically invaluable survey, which included the townlands of Ballymacarrett and Ballyhackamore. The Raven Maps distinguish forty-two houses in the latter, many of which were at the current junction of the Belmont and Holywood Roads. Ballymacarrett reveals only eleven houses which, apart from that of Robert Hunter (perhaps close to the site of Avoniel), were mainly poor cottages.

Topographically, East Belfast rises gently from a narrow coastal plain towards the fertile glacial sands of Knock and the Castlereagh foothills which, at their highest point, are 599 feet above sea level (mean elevation, 405 feet). The lack of pronounced high contours in Ballymacarrett adds a touch of irony to the location of the merchant family's description of their property as Mount Pottinger. The principal characteristic of the entire district in the 16th and 17th centuries was woodland, punctuated by occasional clearings. A map of the coast of Co Down c.1566 - echoed in a further one of 1590 - described the area as densely wooded, with hazel, holly, elder, thorn, crab and birch, very little of this being suitable for construction purposes.

Nevertheless, there was evidently a number of tenants living in Ballymacarrett in the first quarter of the 17th century, as the lease of 1644 for the townland catalogues the many "appurtenances" by which the second Viscount Clandeboye - corpulent, but more easy-going than his father - exploited his tenants: "royalties, tithes, heriots, fines, amercements, woods, underwoods, suits, services, customs, anchorages, fishings ... mills, mill-steads, mill-ponds and water-courses". Raven's map also delineates a salt marsh on the Ballymacarrett shoreline, which was still productive in the mid-19th century.

Ballymacarrett was also becoming the focus of increasing traffic, and a ferry service was established close to the Connswater estuary, which plied its route across the muddy Lagan to a point near High Street. The so-called Con O'Neill bridge in Beersbridge was probably on the track down to the ferry from the Castlereagh Hills. Although it is difficult to date, another point of access from Ballymacarrett to Belfast was a ford across the Lagan between the two present bridges. This was reached by a paved road (now the lower Woodstock Road) from Gooseberry Corner, where, as locally-raised Prof John Wilson Foster described it, "the Woodstock Road collides with the Beersbridge Road". In 1848 Francis Ritchie, who had recently constructed both the Queen's Bridge (as a replacement for the Long Bridge) and the Lagan Bridge (built in basalt stone from Gilnahirk), testified with others that whilst working on the projects he had discovered, between those two crossings, a 25 foot wide causeway of loose stones, of which he had removed several lighter loads.

On 3 April 1624 Viscount Clandeboye leased the townland of Ballymacarrett to Richard and Henry Whitehead for twenty-one years. A certain Richard Pierson then acquired the lease for seven years, up to All Saints 1650. On 15 October 1644, the lease (excepting certain reservations made by the Viscount, recently created 1st Earl of Clanbrassil) was offered to a Scottish merchant and burgess of Ayr, William Kelso, for twenty-one years to begin in 1650 - or sooner if agreed by all parties - at an annual rent of £32, plus six days' work of a man and horse.

On 16 September 1669 Henry, the 2nd Earl of Clanbrassil, granted the lease of Ballymacarrett to John Kelso of that townland for 61 years for the sum of £300. John appears to have enjoyed greater privileges than did his name-sake. It did not include the Owen O'Cork mill or six acres of land attached to the latter, but Kelso did benefit from the fishing rights, the liberty of the ferry-boat, together with the houses, meres and marshes with all their appurtenances.

Within a very short space of time Kelso's interest appears to have been acquired by Captain James Magill of Ballyminestragh. However, on 4 July 1672 he was bought out by the Belfast merchant Thomas Pottinger. Twenty days later the Earl of Clanbrassil effectively sold all his interest in the townland to Pottinger for £300 and an annual payment of £30. This also included the valuable Owen O'Cork corn mill and twelve acres of land (six acres each in Ballymacarrett and Ballyhackamore) then in the possession of John Wilson. The mill was lucrative because the inhabitants not merely of the latter two townlands were obliged to use its facilities, but also those of Knock, Strandtown, Ballycloghan and other adjacent townlands; you could go to another mill, but only on payment of a fine (mulcture) to the owner of Owen O'Cork!

Thomas Pottinger

Born in the Orkney Islands, Thomas Pottinger made part of his fortune as a merchant and agent in the West Indies for George Macartney of Belfast in the 1660s. He was appointed Sovereign of Belfast in 1688-89, and probably saved the city from destruction by opening its gates to James II in the latter year, but he was to assist William III's general, Schomberg, later that same year.

The growth of traffic between Belfast and Co Down was reflected in the construction of the Long Bridge in Scrabo stone during the 1680s. It was almost 800 metres in length, much of which was taken up by spanning the extensive mudflats at that point, as eighteen of its twenty-one arches were officially in Ballymacarrett. After landing at Ballyholme in August 1689, Schomberg - who was to die at the Battle of the Boyne - yomped across the bridge on his way to Carrickfergus, and in the spring of 1692 seven arches eventually collapsed, it was claimed, "having been weakened by Duke Schomberg drawing his heavy cannon over it some time before as well as by a ship driving against it".

There was clearly some nervousness on the town (Co Antrim) side of the Lagan about the aspirations of the Pottinger family, for when Thomas died in 1717 to be succeeded by his son Joseph - who was astute enough to marry the daughter of the Earl of Dundonald - Arthur, the Earl of Donegall, placed stakes along the river to demarcate his property from that of the owners of Mount Pottinger.

Despite his adventurous background, Thomas Pottinger seems to have lacked any real vision for Ballymacarrett. He sub-let some of his property, such as a 15 acre farm to James Biggar (at £3 13s - or £3.65 - per annum), but by the mid-18th century the only substantial property in the area was the family home and the Owen O'Cork mill. The first real visionary to develop the potential of Ballymacarrett was Barry Yelverton - later Lord Avonmore - born in Co Cork, who purchased it from Eldred Pottinger in 1779 for £18,113 5s. Yelverton has been described as "mean and common in appearance, with manners devoid of dignity, and curiously absent-minded".

However, he was blessed with rhetorical skills and a sharp mind, and it may have been the latter, plus the fact that he was born into penurious circumstances, which helped him to appreciate the commercial advantages of his acquisition.

Barry Yelverton

The prevailing rural character of Ballymacarrett at this stage can be discerned from the fact that the many exploitable features purchased by Yelverton were almost identical to those specified in the 1644 lease. Nevertheless, it was during Yelverton's ownership that the first industries were established in the townland. In the early 1780s both Benjamin Edwards and John Smylie commenced glass manufacturing at Bridge End, and Edwards contemporaneously formed an iron foundry at the junction of what became Newtownards Road and Foundry Row, making bottle moulds, boilers and grinding machines, as well as domestic goods. On 26 November 1783 Yelverton leased eleven acres to William Seed, which included the Owen O'Cork mill (whose name probably derives from the Irish *abhain coirce* - the oat mill at the river), and converted it to a flour mill.

Yelverton started to reclaim the mud-flats (or slob-land) close to Bridge End, lay out streets, and - to encourage economic development - to grant leases in perpetuity.

Arthur, 5th Earl of Donegall (created Marquis in 1791) - who refused to grant improving leases even to established tenants, and often sold them to the highest bidder - interpreted this as a direct challenge. Emulating his predecessor Sir Arthur Chichester at the end of the 16th century, who had hired the rootless and landless natives to plunder and harass the tenants of the Earl of Tyrone, the contemporary Arthur in 1786 used a gang of wreckers to destroy Yelverton's embankments in an effort to flood the improvements. The Cork man was not intimidated, and Donegall, on 1 July 1787, felt it incumbent upon him to buy out his rival at a cost of £25,000.

The Donegall Family

The onset of the 19th century witnessed an acceleration in the industrialisation of East Belfast, echoing progress in Great Britain. The financial complications of the Donegall family were a catalyst for this development. Seven years before his death in 1799 the first Marquis had married for the third time. His wife, Barbara Godfrey, was very young, and in his will he left her an annuity of £1000 to be paid from his Ballymacarrett estates. Whilst this in itself may not have proved too crippling, he died with debts of fourteen times his annual income, at £400,000. His profligate habits, and his failure to pay any of his debts if he could possibly avoid them, led him to become known as the Marquis of 'Done-em-all', and his descendants had no choice but to raise income by the provision of more and more leases from their property.

In his will, the first Marquis bequeathed Ballymacarrett to his second son, Lord Spencer Stanley Chichester, whose successors became Baron Templemore, whose plans to create a planned urban area were only partially successful. Chichester resented his father's arrangements for his step-mother, and there were to be disagreeable episodes. In July 1815 Barbara, the Dowager Marchioness, celebrated Wellington's recent victory at Waterloo by winning litigation against her step-son, which obliged him to let for three years "all that lot of ground known by the name of Lot 30 or Ewing's Holding, containing eight acres situate on the right and left sides of the road leading to Newtownards in the townland of Ballymacarrett".

In the 1860s Henry Spencer, Baron Templemore, was receiving an annual rental of £1000, but it was claimed that this was only a fraction of the actual value, listed in the 1855 Poor Law rate books at nearly £19,000 per annum - a massive increase on the annual value of £4 enjoyed by Sir James Hamilton in the 1620s!

The development of East Belfast proceeded fitfully in the first half of the 19th century, and then accelerated rapidly. The signs of demographic expansion, a resident population - which by the mid-19th century totalled approximately 10,500 in Ballymacarrett, Ballyhackamore and Knockbreda - were many. Gas illumination was projected for the town side of the Long Bridge in the 1820s, and by 1830 the multiplying traffic over this bridge resulted in a large fissure appearing in it, which necessitated £20,000 worth of repairs. Even this proved cosmetic, and in 1842 a new span (soon afterwards renamed the Queen's Bridge) was built, and in the same decade the Lagan (or Coates, and later Albert) Bridge - up to that stage a toll bridge - was purchased. These two crossings fed the arteries that led to the embryonic Albertbridge and Newtownards Roads.

From the mid 19th century the immense injection of labour and commerce carpeted the townlands of East Belfast. The transformation of Ballymacarrett into Ireland's most industrialised 575 acres has left its scars - both on the landscape and on the inhabitants.

The building of three churches so close to each other close to the King's Road and Knock Road junction between 1870 and 1890 is an undoubted signal of a flourishing resident population in the district.

By 1870 the growing band of Methodists at Knock had to travel some distance to the nearest church in Ballymacarrett, later destroyed by the Luftwaffe in 1941. Consequently "a very neat and commodious church" was built of plain red and white brick at Green Road on the site of the current church hall.

It was dedicated on 13 January 1870. It was illuminated by two pendants from the ceiling, each sporting three oil lamps of white glass; there were matching wall brackets, and two oil lamps on the pulpit which provided further illumination from that point! Within a decade the church membership - some of whom came to worship on horseback - had increased from 41 to 245, and a new church built from distinctive Scrabo sandstone was opened on 13 June 1883 beside the original building. It displayed a shamrock motif on the façade as a symbol of the Trinity.

Amongst the worshippers were William Hinde, a coal merchant and ship owner, who lived about one hundred yards distant at Brooklyn - where the current RUC HQ is now based - and Thomas Pullman, a handkerchief manufacturer, who resided two doors beyond there at Rosemount. J J Shillington, who ran a factory on Broadway, travelled to worship from Glenmachan Tower off the Belmont Road.

Opinions will always vary, but not everyone was enamoured of the Knock congregation. The dour and controversial Rev Charles Inwood was incumbent for only one year in 1894, but his memoirs indicate that, although there was a wealthy congregation in his pews, he felt that they were "not possessed of much out-and-out religion ... They do not seem to understand what 'holiness' means"!

However, these men were typical of the Victorian businessmen who believed that the puritanical virtues of punctuality, industry and piety brought prosperity in their wake. Methodists were at the forefront of demands for abstinence and, as much as anyone, would have sensed the opportunities presented by the establishment of Stormont, scarcely a mile distant. Within a couple of years of the parliament (then in Belfast) opening, they had managed to dispose of the scourge of the spirit grocers.

Increasing membership necessitated extensions being made to the church in 1925. A new gallery, transepts, organ chamber, vestry, choir room, entrance and porch were dedicated on 9 November 1925 by those stalwarts of Ulster Methodism, Lady Kelly and her husband, Sir Samuel. Knock Methodist Church now contains one of the most colourful arrays of stained glass in East Belfast.

Knock Methodist Church
Green Road

MARTIN D. COOKE
UWS

Racing at Ballyhackamore has been replaced by racing through Ballyhackamore! For many commuters, the village is simply a convenient reference point on their journey to and from Belfast but, for those who live in the community, there is considerable pride taken in their efforts to retain the 'village' atmosphere. Ballyhackamore retained its rural dimension long after Ballymacarrett had become industrialised.

The origin of the name has long been disputed; some claim that it means 'the townland of the big horses', but more authoritative sources claim it may mean 'townland of the mud flats' (as its boundary may once have been adjacent to the Lough).

Samuel Elliott, who lived on the Cregagh Road in the early 19th century, has bequeathed us a vibrant account of the Christmas fair at Ballyhackamore in the first half of the 19th century. Horse-racing and steeple-chasing off the Sandown Road were a central feature of the festivities:

On this occasion thousands of people assembled from Belfast and the adjacent towns and surrounding country districts. Tents and booths were pitched all over the immediate fields, in which refreshments of the worst possible quality were to be obtained at the highest possible prices. Shooting galleries, aunt sallies, wheels of fortune ... ginger beer stalls, combined with numerous basket-women, laden with cakes, toffee and barley-sugar. In addition to all this, add the adornments of the various coloured flags ... and the clamour and noise of thousands of men, women boys and girls, some of them bettors on the race ... [this gives you] an idea of the scenes enacted at Ballyhackamore on Christmas Day.

Elliott recalled that the two Robinson brothers of Castlereagh were "about the most turf-sporting men of those days in Ireland". In 1799 the Belfast News Letter recorded that there were races at Ballyhackamore from 9 to 13 December. These had been adjourned until 9 December "at the request of several sportsmen and gentlemen, and to have moonlight" - the latter presumably for the benefit of fair-goers. The winners included Mr Chichester's *Spangle* and Mr Pottinger's *Farewell*; the latter did gain one walk-over, but he also defeated the chestnut *Mary Queen of Scots* over four miles.

Another winner was *Ramjam*, who had previously raced at the Maze and Newmarket. He was a fine dark brown colour, and boasted good bone features and a fine temper, which he inherited from his sire, *Diamond*. The latter features in a painting in 1800 by George Stubbs now at Mount Stewart, being beaten by the never-beaten *Hambletonian* at Newmarket in the same year.

Ballyhackamore

Although vegetarians will disagree, all self-respecting villages require their butcher. Ballyhackamore is no exception. In the early 20th century, one such trader, Mr J G Smart (of Sinclair Buildings, nearly opposite Earlswood Road), lived up to his name. One local resident of Knock recalled that "Mr Smart, the butcher in Ballyhackamore, who kept hackney ponies, delivered his wares in an elegant turn-out".

The row of shops which includes William McCambley's Select Cuts (between Earlswood Road and Eastleigh Drive) was originally the site until the late 1920s of three villas - Rossville, Sandiacre and Eastleigh. Thomas Rudnick's butcher's shop had appeared in 1932; by 1940 the business had been purchased by W J Hall, who in turn sold out to John Irwin. William McCambley acquired the business in the mid-1980s.

Even in this latter period, Mr McCambley brought in carcasses and displayed them on the rails, which are still visible around the shop, for customers to select their cuts. There was also a rail beneath the current neon sign, beneath which the floor still slopes away to the street, where the blood was enabled to drain away.

In the early 1990s Mr McCambley opened a delicatessen on the other side of the road (opposite Earlswood Road), separating the cooked and raw meat trade - even ahead of European regulations!

One of the current businesses which prepares such dishes is award-winning Alden's restaurant, opened in 1998 at the junction with Sandown Road. The owner, Jonathan Davis, named the establishment after his boarding house at Campbell College which, in turn, was named after one of the earliest masters at the school - Lewis Alden. The latter's expert teaching was acknowledged by four professors, including C S Lewis. The white-haired, short-sighted English teacher was renowned by his nickname, Octie, because when roused to anger his eyes would reputedly swell like those of an octopus. How appropriate if Alden's were to include this on the menu!

Many traders of the first half of this century delivered by horse and cart, such as bread salesmen and milkmen. One vital supporting business for this was the blacksmith, and before the First World War farrier work was undertaken by the blacksmith, Edward McAnally, whose forge was at Vulcan Terrace (opposite the present-day library). Whilst this profession has long since vanished from the suburban streets, there are those like William McCambley who prefer to believe that Ballyhackamore is a place "where tradition is not a thing of the past".

McCambley's Select Cuts
BALLYHACKAMORE

Harland & Wolff's work with oil rigs has been embraced partly to compensate for the decline in the shipping trade. However, the success of the company - once the largest and most successful in the world - was based from the start in 1861 on the adventurous and creative genius of one of its founders, Edward Harland.

The one thing which the author of this book has in common with Edward Harland is that they were both born in Scarborough on the Yorkshire coast! Some of Harland's designs were inspired by the sea. Rivals predicted that his longer, sharper designs were too fragile for maritime travel, but they were ultimately to prove the foundation of his success. The ship-builder claimed that he had taken the hint from nature, which "seems to have furnished us with the finest design for a vessel in the form of a fish; it presents such fine lines, is so clean, so true and so rapid in its movements".

Another of Harland's characteristics was attention to detail. It was said of him that "a bit of chalk was ever in his vest pocket; he made a white circle round any defect he would see in the workshops ... Another constant companion was an ivory foot rule. Disciplinarian as he was [he sacked anyone caught smoking], he was nevertheless just ... He carried his head erect, as will be seen by his statue in the grounds of City Hall". He was equally fastidious about his clothes; he kept a plaster-cast for his footwear, and once sent back a dozen new hand-made shirts because they were half an inch too long! It was said that the *Majestic* launched by

Harland & Wolff in 1889 was named after his character and deportment.

Produced in the same year, *Teutonic* was named in honour of Harland's partner, Gustav Wolff, who also helped to found the Belfast Ropeworks Co on the Newtownards Road in 1875. Despite living in East Belfast for over 50 years he never lost his German accent. Wolff, who resided at The Den on Station Road in Sydenham, was more the financier, and a little more relaxed than his partner. He displayed his modesty and good humour when asked to make a speech during the trials of a new steamer: "Sir Edward Harland builds the ships; Mr Pirrie makes the speeches, and as for me I smoke cigars for the firm"! This phlegmatic approach was needed on occasions. In India in 1887, buying supplies of jute and sisal, he complained of the price of his ticket on the sleeper to Allahabad. The railway staff retaliated by uncoupling his coach, and left him stranded!

Harland & Wolff
Queen's Island

MARTIN D COOKE
U.W.S.

The pastoral ambience of Campbell College belies the occasionally turbulent events which have encompassed it over the years.

When it opened its doors on 3 September 1894, the Trustees of Henry Campbell (who owned the Mossley Mills) had appointed joint-Headmasters, both seduced from Methodist College in 1890. Henry Richard Parker, an Episcopalian, and James Adams McNeill, an entrenched Presbyterian, clashed persistently, and denominational tensions resulted in the departure of the former within a year.

These events alienated the staff, and by the end of the second academic year seven of the original thirteen staff had been encouraged or forced to resign. A subsequent 'pamphlet war' between the staff and McNeill resulted in a celebrated court case in Dublin for slander and libel. Although the ousted member of staff - Andrew Boyd, who went on to become a clergyman, and died in his vestry at Inver Parish Church in Larne in June 1925 - won the case, he was awarded only £5 in damages. Everyone back at the Belmont estate felt it expedient to regard this as a great victory for the headmaster, and his carriage was pulled in celebration from the main gates to the front of the school, and bonfires were lit in the grounds!

On the evening of 27 December 1935, the College was attacked by the IRA, attempting to steal the rifles of the Officer Training Corps (now the CCF). The police had prior information about the raid, which proved to be mishandled by the intruders. A gunfight ensued in the Hawthornden Road gate lodge between three IRA gunmen and a lone policeman. Despite the presence of ten people (including the gate lodge occupants) in one small room, only the policeman suffered injuries. Constable Hay survived two bullet wounds, and was consequently promoted to sergeant!

During the Second World War the College was evacuated to the Northern Counties Hotel (now rebuilt as the Comfort Hotel) in Portrush, and the Belmont estate was commissioned as General Hospital no. 24. On the night of 4/5 May 1941, as the Luftwaffe turned out of Belfast towards Stormont, a number of bombs were dropped on the school, resulting in some structural damage and the death of nineteen doctors and patients.

Former pupils of Campbell College include Mike Gibson, the most-capped Irish rugby international; Gordon Burns, creator of *The Krypton Factor*; Charles Lawson, Jim McDonald of *Coronation Street*; and Squadron Leader Terry Bulloch, DSO and bar, DFC and bar, the most successful anti-submarine air ace of the Second World War.

Campbell College
BELMONT

From 1650 one minister was given charge of two Presbyterian congregations at Knock and Breda. Seventy years later, under Rev Francis Montgomery, they were united. The new congregation was renamed Castlereagh, and a church built on the present site. It is not beyond the bounds of possibility that the stone used in the construction of this first church was quarried from the empty castle of Con O'Neill, which stood about 100 yards distant.

The parish had very wide boundaries when Rev Henry Haslett succeeded as minister (aged only 23) in September 1816, ministering to nearly 800 families. The church became too cramped, so Haslett built a new one in 1834 (for £1400). It seated 800 parishioners, but after six months it started to collapse and had to be rebuilt! The new Castlereagh Meeting House was officially opened with a service on 16 August 1835 and, in view of that near collapse, there must have been a few chuckles in the congregation at the sermon based on Matthew 16, v.18: "You are Peter, and upon this rock I will build my church"!

A new minister, Rev William Rogers, was ordained on 29 May 1871. In their efforts to call a new minister, the congregation may well have been intrigued by his bold choice of sermons; his first trial homily on 1 January 1871 was on 'The Ten Virgins'; deterred by appalling weather, the congregation on this occasion was small, so they asked him back in March when he spoke on 'The Pharisee and the Publican'!

Rogers was an anguished but earnest soul, and in the first three years of his mission cared for his widespread parish whilst living four miles distant at his aunt's home at Strandtown Villa (on the Holywood Road). He was a popular figure, despite the dour philosophy that his biographer revealed: "young people soon saw that life was a serious business, that there was little room in it for play or amusement, that hard work and prayer and worship were the only fit occupations for rational people"! His congregation appears to have responded positively, for in reflective mood Rogers declared Co Down people to be very kind-hearted: "the outstanding characteristic of the Castlereagh people from generation to generation".

There are families from many parts of East Belfast buried in the Castlereagh graveyard. The saddest must be that of Philip Campbell who erected a memorial to his five sisters who died between 1853 and 1899, all outlived by their mother, who died in 1901. Three also pre-deceased their father, who passed away in 1872.

Times change and, considering the volume of traffic which now hurtles by this church, there must be regret at the disappearance of a relaxed pace of life when Rogers reflected: "Time was not measured by city clocks in Castlereagh".

Castlereagh
Presbyterian Church

The original Rosepark villa stood facing Stormont House (later Stormont Castle) of the Cleland family across what is now the Upper Newtownards Road. Rosepark was built in 1830 for Octavia Crawford of Cabin Hill. She and her three sisters were bequeathed £4000 each by their father, Hugh Crawford, a banker who lived at Orangefield, and she brought her portion to her marriage. In May 1833 Octavia married Lt-Col Dunlop Digby (of Clifden House, Galway) who had been present at the trial in 1798 of Rev James Porter of Greyabbey. Digby later recorded that, when the sentence of hanging was pronounced on the minister, there were "tears in my eyes as I left the court".

As one of those who presided at Porter's trial was the unscrupulous Rev John Cleland, it is intriguing to contemplate what Digby's attitude was towards his neighbour and landlord! Octavia described Rosepark in 1847 as having "a parlour and drawing room, each 22 feet by 18 feet, four good bedrooms and dressing closet, two large garrets, cellars under the parlour, and an excellent walled garden and choice fruit".

After her husband died at Rosepark on 9 July 1846, Octavia appears to have had problems disposing of the property, and in 1848 she enquired from England as to whether the Clelands at Stormont had shown any interest in purchasing it - otherwise, she indicated, she would have to hire some grazers and sow some oats to pay for the ground rent owed to her neighbours. She was not complimentary of her landlords, commenting that "Money is God to the Clelands"! It may be that the Clelands did acquire the house, as one Samuel Jackson Cleland is reported to have been killed when one of the walls of Rosepark, which he was demolishing, fell on him and killed him!

The name of Rosepark is retained in the housing development which emerged in the area of the original house between 1934 and 1938. The particular house featured is 6 Rosepark East, the home of the artist of this book. It was completed in August 1936 with art deco interior by the builder Robert Hewitt, as a wedding present for his son James (a loss adjuster), who was to occupy it for over sixty years.

James, who was interested in guns, fishing and photography, married Enid. Robert Hewitt, who operated from his workshops at 50 Sandown Road from the early years of the 20th century - and was the effective builder of much of Ballyhackamore - named Hewitt Parade and Enid Parade (off Holland Drive) as a memorial to his son and daughter-in-law.

6 Rosepark East
UPPER NEWTOWNARDS ROAD

MARTIN D. COOKE
UWS

The first cinema built in Belfast for commercial purposes was the Electric in York Street, opened in 1910. This prompted the establishment in the following year of the first cinema in Ballymacarrett - the Picturedrome on the Mountpottinger Road. This was followed in the same decade by the Princess Picture House (or Old Princess), the New Princess, the Willowfield and the Popular (or Pop).

By the 1930s the fact that they boasted wall-to-wall carpet, comfortable chairs, a bright environment and central heating - accompanied by the introduction of sound - made them a welcome release from the drab reality of the Depression years. The 1930s also witnessed in East Belfast the addition of the Castle, the Astoria, the Ambassador and the Strand.

In the post-First World War years of high unemployment, James Craig, the Prime Minister, was disturbed to see so many soldiers wandering aimlessly through the streets, and suggested opening the cinemas for them on Sundays. However, his General Officer Commanding for the district retorted that he would place them out of bounds if they dared to open on the Lord's Day!

The Strand was opened by the Lord Mayor, Sir Crawford McCullagh, on 7 December 1935 on the site of the castellated Strandtown House, the former home of shipping company owner, Sir Gustavus Heyn. The cinema offered 1170 seats (900 in the stalls, and 270 in the more expensive 1s 6d [8p] balcony).

The entrance was flat-iron shaped, and it sported 'snake' design carpeting. The electrical installation by Lewers, Carroll & Co - surely there must have been Alice in Wonderland quips about that company name! - illuminated the stage curtain in any colour or combination of colours from 1500 light points. At the official opening it was commented upon that the interior triple deck of porthole lights, appropriately for East Belfast, reflected that of an ocean liner.

The first manager at the Strand was Harry Buckley, who had formerly been at the Coliseum. The first of very many films was *Bright Eyes*, starring Shirley Temple. The supporting programme was a comedy starring Ernie Lotinga entitled *Smith and Wives*, a colour cartoon entitled *Babes at Sea*, and the Movietone News. The first change on the following Thursday saw Gracie Fields in *Look Up and Laugh*.

After some uncertain years the Strand closed on 19 November 1983, and became briefly a concert and variety theatre which featured, amongst others, George Jones. In 1994 it re-opened successfully as a four-screen cinema - the only cinema remaining in East Belfast.

Strand Cinema
HOLYWOOD ROAD

All houses have a story to tell, but few can have generated as many intriguing - even fantastic - tales as Little Lea on Circular Road. This is the home built in the early years of the 20th century by Belfast solicitor Albert Lewis. His son, the celebrated author C S (Jack) Lewis - only seven at the time - was later rather caustic, and claimed that "My father, who had more capacity for being cheated than any man I know, was badly cheated by his builders; the drains were wrong, the chimneys were wrong, and there was a draught in every room".

When C S Lewis and his family moved in, it was an unspoiled area with relatively few neighbours. These included, on the other side of the road, the Greeves family at Bernagh, whom Jack befriended, and Craigavon, then the home of James Craig junior. Closer to the Holywood Road, in a house built later, lived J L Stewart, who opened the first of his numerous cash stores on the Beersbridge Road near the junction with Bloomfield, opposite St Donard's Church.

That Jack became a story writer is probably no surprise. His grandfather, Richard Lewis - who founded the Belfast boilermakers, engineers and iron shipbuilders, MacIlwaine and Lewis - composed fantasy stories to entertain his children. His son, Albert, was inordinately fond of relating what he termed 'wheezes' - improbable and bizarre, but true, stories of Ulster life - the best of which unfortunately cannot be re-told here, but may be found in the pages of A N Wilson's biography of C S Lewis!

The whole district and local scenery, including the hills of County Down where Jack Lewis walked, remained in the affections of the Christian author, and in 1941, when the Luftwaffe dropped bombs along the Belmont Road and on Campbell College, he wrote to Arthur Greeves that "It's like the end of the world to think of bombs near Schomberg" (on the Belmont Road, owned by the Greeves family).

Surprisingly, Jack never felt affectionate towards Little Lea, except the Little End Room, in which he and his brother Warren (or Warnie) escaped from the adult world around them. A wardrobe carved by his grandfather - now in Chicago - was the inspiration for one of his *Chronicles of Narnia*, 'The Lion, the Witch and the Wardrobe', which may even be based upon an episode in the early life of his mother. There are those who would also argue that the Lion was impressed upon his imagination by his visits to his maternal grandmother's church, St Mark's, where the doorpull on the Old Rectory was in the shape of a lion's head.

Little Lea

CIRCULAR ROAD, BELMONT

It was only towards the end of last century that, even amongst the majority of local inhabitants, many people came to recognise that one of the century's most notable literary giants hailed from East Belfast.

Various events were scheduled to commemorate and celebrate the centenary of C S Lewis's birth on 29 November 1898. A trail was devised to encompass many of the locations in East Belfast associated with his early life, such as his homes (Dundela Villas, and Little Lea), his school (Campbell College) and his church (St Mark's).

In November 1998 a bronze memorial, sculpted by Ross Wilson, was inaugurated by Lewis's step-son, Douglas Gresham, outside the new Holywood Arches Library, at a spot underneath where the Belfast & County Down Railway arches used to run. There is a certain appropriateness about the location, for the author was later to describe his one term at Campbell College, in late 1910, as "very much like living permanently in a large railway station"! This reflected the eleven year old's overwhelming impression of an intimidating, impersonal and noisy environment.

One of his marginally older boarding contemporaries at the school, E R Dodds - who, like Lewis, was to become an Oxford professor - also recalled the ethos of the school with little affection. Dodds described the headmaster, R A H MacFarland, as "a fat man of unpleasing appearance whose superfluous flesh quivered like a jelly". He was expelled for effectively chastising the headmaster, but failed in his ulti-mate ambition which was to waylay MacFarland on the back lane of the school which leads to the Belmont Road, in order to tar and feather him!

The bronze sculpture depicts Digory Kirke, one of Lewis's characters from *The Chronicles of Narnia*, tentatively entering a large Victorian wardrobe. Kirke - perhaps intended to be the alter ego of the author - was one of the first characters in the series to visit Narnia, and grew up to become Professor Kirke in The Lion, the Witch and the Wardrobe.

C S Lewis Memoria

THE ARCHE

Partly because of some members of the congregation, C S Lewis (known as Jack) never displayed much affection for St Mark's, where his maternal grandfather - Rev Thomas Hamilton - had been the first rector from 1878 to 1900. However, the Lewis family continues to cast its colourful light upon the church, for in the south aisle there are memorial stained-glass windows both to Jack's parents and his grandfather.

Built on Bunker Hill, St Mark's replaced an earlier place of worship which stood on the site of the present Tesco's supermarket at Gelston's Corner. It was designed by William Butterfield, but there is no evidence that it was ever visited by its architect. One of its main benefactors was another of C S Lewis's relations - the linen manufacturer Sir William Ewart, whom the author referred to as 'Cousin Quartus'.

Four of its first eight rectors were elevated to the episcopate, including the present Archbishop of Armagh, the Most Rev Robin Eames. One of the primate's predecessors at Dundela, Rev Arthur Barton, was promoted to the archdiocese of Dublin in 1939. Blessed with a sense of humour and of occasion, Barton (in his guise as a Governor) had been asked in 1929 to inaugurate the new Campbell College swimming pool, then in the grounds of Ormiston. He followed a speech 'of commendable aptness and brevity' by suddenly dispensing with his clerical garb and executing 'a competent dive'!

One of the first pew rents to be paid at St Mark's was that of the Smiles family of Westbank, situated adjacently in Palmerston Road. In 1875, on the Newtownards Road, William Holmes Smiles had founded the Belfast Ropework Co, which even sold rope to the celebrated tightrope walker, Charles Blondin. Smiles did not attend worship regularly at St Mark's, appearing usually only at the christenings of his eleven children. He was the son of Dr Samuel Smiles, the author of the Victorian classic *Self Help*, and one tale is told which reflects the inspiration of his father's noted principle. He had given a coin to each of his children before a church service to donate to the collection on behalf of a hospital. Discovering that it was actually to pay for an employee of the hospital, he instructed his children to hold on to the money when the collection plate was circulated - although one of his daughters did show defiance!

Every Saturday the steeple of St Mark's witnessed the entire Smiles family - all thirteen of them - depart, with father in the van, for their invariable cycle ride from Strandtown to Newtownards, Bangor and Donaghadee.

St Mark's Church
Dundela

As the townland of Ballymacarrett became increasingly populated and industrialised, the factory owners and entrepreneurs sought to build their mansions on the higher, more salubrious plateau of Knock, Strandtown and Belmont.

One of the first houses in the area - which gave its name to the district - was Belmont, occupied in the 1860s by (later Sir) Thomas McClure, who owned much land in the area. He leased out land to the architect Thomas Jackson, who proceeded to design such mansions as Glenmachan Towers, Craigavon, Lismachan and - originally as his own home - Altona.

However, one residence, designed in the mid 1860s, which manifested a different style was Ormiston, adjacent to Belmont. This was designed in the Scottish Baronial style (akin to that of Stormont Castle) by the Edinburgh architect David Bryce. It was comissioned by the Belfast businessman James Combe, who had originally come from Scotland, and it is said that he named it (with a slight modification) after his mother's birth-place in Scotland, Orbiston.

Ormiston was later purchased by Sir Edward Harland, who had previously resided along the Belmont Road at Edenvale (close to the junction with Holywood Road), whose name is retained in local street names. The most notable occupants of Ormiston were Lord and Lady Pirrie, who installed a nine-hole golf course in the grounds. The house was sold in 1927, three years after Pirrie's death, to

Campbell College as a junior boarding house, as which it remained until it was sold in 1974 to the Police Authority. (The name of Ormiston is retained at Campbell College in a brick and glass building, now a classroom block).

Ormiston witnessed tentative military action in 1913 following the establishment of the Ulster Volunteer Force at nearby Craigavon; Sir Spencer Chichester permitted the East Belfast contingents of the UVF to drill and train in the grounds of Ormiston. These men included the three sons of Rev John MacDermott - minister at Belmont Presbyterian Church - one of whom, Clarke, was to become, with great irony, Minister for Public Security in 1940-41 and a future Lord Chief Justice of Northern Ireland.

During the 1920s, Campbell College installed an indoor range for its Officer Training Corps shooting teams, and during the Second World War - when the school became a military hospital - Ormiston was designated as quarters for nurses.

Sadly, it now stands empty and mouldering.

ORMISTON
HAWTHORNDEN ROAD

Family connections were particularly important at Harland & Wolff; loyal service to the company could ensure the employment of the next generation at Queen's Island.

Such associations were equally valuable at the higher echelons of the company. Although rather distantly, Edward Harland and Gustav Wolff were related, and it was this factor which enabled Harland to finance his venture.

Two others, who both became Managing Directors at the ship-yard, were Alexander Montgomery Carlisle and Thomas Andrews - chief designer and a victim of the *Titanic*. The latter was a nephew, and Carlisle a brother-in-law, of the Chairman of Harland & Wolff, Viscount Pirrie. However, the latter never offered favours on the grounds of nepotism. Carlisle was eventually to resign, probably because of Pirrie's dictatorial manner, and Thomas Andrews died on the *Titanic*, because at the last minute he replaced Pirrie, who was in poor health.

Someone who knew Pirrie as a boy in Comber said that "no-one would have guessed at the astuteness hidden under that very common-place and rather silly exterior". Pirrie was exceptionally successful at running Harland & Wolff, and his energetic, shrewd and audacious character was an indisputable reason. He was an exceptional salesman with the requisite ready smile.

However, he was also extremely ruthless and egostistical. It was said that he was at his most dangerous when apparently most cordial. One senior director, who had been treated most affably at a meeting, only realised after he left the office that he had, in fact, been sacked! Pirrie was manipulative, and even his six Managing Directors (including nephew Thomas) feared him. He was secretive about the affairs of the company, and ensured that his senior officials never knew everything about the business, and certainly not enough to threaten his control.

His methods of doing business - even if fundamentally pursued to ensure full order books - were often dubious, if not unscrupulous. He became extremely wealthy - owning a house in the West End of London, a 2800 acre estate in Surrey, as well as his Belfast residence of Ormiston. Yet for all his wealth, he mismanaged his own finances so ineffectually that, when he died in 1924, he was almost destitute, and left Lady Pirrie in parlous circumstances.

Pumps are used for various purposes, including operating a company's machinery and the removal of dross and impurities. The Old Pump House is perhaps an appropriate symbol of Pirrie's management of Harland & Wolff.

Old Pump Room

HARLAND & WOLFF

Knockdene Park - close to the junction of the Upper Newtownards and Knock Roads - first makes an appearance in the pages of the Belfast Street Directory in the early 20th century. Two of the first houses were Alona, occupied by tea merchant David Bell, whose family still have their shop - S D Bell's - at the Knock junction, and Astolat, built by John Milliken (to whom there is a memorial window in St Columba's Parish Church on King's Road). The latter was for many years Secretary to the Belfast & County Down Railway, and had had to deal with the correspondence and litigation relating to the 1871 Ballymacarrett Rail Accident.

Honor Rudnitsky, who was raised on the Knockdene estate, later wrote that "for all its sleepy tranquillity, I think Knock must have produced more oddities to the square acre than any other place on earth". One of these was the noted artist, J W (Joseph) Carey. He designed the house, Brugh, in which he lived from 1906 to 1937, where the family lived out their "warm, chaotic and bohemian" existence.

Carey had worked for the printing company Marcus Ward until its collapse in 1895, the same year in which he wandered the Castlereagh Hills to sketch the remains of Con O'Neill's castle. He was an absent-minded individual, who often failed to remember what he had just eaten for dinner, but was mentally sharp enough to defeat the Cuban world chess champion, Capablanca, during a simultaneous display in Belfast in 1924.

The Careys were a naturally hospitable couple. Their garden acted, inadvertently, as a virtual public right of way, and their house - as well as giving a liberal home to a free-ranging parrot named Lorita, and a similarly motivated Persian cat named Angela - offered considerable hospitality. Their guests included artists of the calibre of William Conor, who had been equally 'bohemian' in his time, and musicians such as Percy French.

As a result of carelessness and a number of miscalculations, Mrs Carey once addressed a women's meeting in Thompson's Restaurant in Belfast, in the presence of Lady Clanwilliam, dressed in a petticoat, which doubled as a black satin evening dress, and lace curtains acting as a pearl white lace shawl!

Honor Rudnitsky, their biographer, summarised their company: "We simply enjoyed the Careys and, possibly because we had all been reared in more conventional households, we relished their unusual way of looking at life. What worried other people never bothered them" - except that Joseph Carey despised dandelions, and was once arrested by the police during the Troubles of the 1920s for wandering into Cabin Hill - then a government office - to dig up the offending weed!

The Careys at Brugh
KNOCKDENE PARK

In 1870 Thomas McClure of Belmont provided the use of the Old Mill (at the junction of Knock Road and Cherryvalley) as a Sunday School for the local community. The local church grew out of this enterprise, and the first communion service was held in September 1872. The foundation stone for the church was laid three years later by McClure, who donated the land, as he had done thirteen years earlier for the sister church at Belmont.

Between the first service in January 1876 and 1921 the church was known as Dundela - which was perhaps derived more from the local villa (opposite Beaconfield) than from the more distant Strandtown district. The original church has been extended twice, and its present design dates from 1907.

The incumbent from 1889 to 1924, Rev James Hunter, was a pioneer of instrumental and musical accompaniment to Presbyterian services. This did not always accord with his contemporaries, some of whom preferred a simplistic, puritanical approach to worship.

One early 20th century minister in Bangor would ask for female members of the congregation to cross their legs, uttering: "Now the gates of Hell are shut"! Another Presbyterian, Rev Prof John Barkley, a former pupil at Campbell College, reflected that there were those whom "even [the angel] Gabriel could not please"; and his fellow Campbellian, son of the great Ballymoney Presbyterian J B Armour, lamented that when listening to some jeremiahs

"one was inclined to ask how God made the world without these people"!

For all his tolerant approach to music, however, Hunter at Knock still seemed to practise strict resistance to temptation - at Sunday School Christmas parties, he placed long benches down the hall to separate girls and boys! Like his contemporary fellow minister, MacDermott at Belmont, he could also indulge in lengthy sermons, and it has been written that "many young worshippers at [his] evening service became impatient long before the whistle of the 8.21 pm train from Knock to Donaghadee on the old Belfast & County Down Railway intimated that in another five minutes or so all would be over"!

Knock
Presbyterian Church
KING'S ROAD/KNOCK ROAD

MARTIN D. COOKE
UWS

Just as life itself is said to have evolved from primeval mud, so the spirit of East Belfast sprang from the slob-lands of the Lagan estuary.

The extent of the latter can be gauged from the memories of the 19th century businessman, Narcissus Batt, who recalled leaving Belfast in the 1830s on a steamer bound for Dublin; when he awoke the following morning he found that the vessel was stuck in the mud where Queen's Island now stands!

In order to develop the port facilities, the Harbour Commissioners in 1841 hired the Irish engineer, William Dargan, to dredge the meandering river estuary. Over half a million tons of mud were piled up to form a seventeen-acre site which originally bore his name, until it was changed to Queen's Island to honour Queen Victoria's four hour visit to Belfast on 11 August 1849.

As early as 1843 the Harbour Commissioners began to plant the island "to create a pleasure ground for public use", as a source of "healthful relaxation to the working classes". Its popularity flourished following a fête in August 1850, which included magicians, Scottish singers, bands and boat races. The day also included the ascent of a Montgolfier balloon, which was spoiled by its miniature size, and a firework display which suffered from unseasonal weather.

In 1851, as an echo of the Crystal Palace in London, a much smaller version was built on the island. 112 feet long, built in glass, iron and wood (total cost £670), it was decorated with a bright blue interior, and littered with crouching lions, giant vases, sculptures and a fountain. During the next few years it became very popular with all classes of society, but it was destroyed by fire in January 1864.

The south-eastern part of Queen's Island had been leased in 1851 to Thompson & Kirwan's shipyard. In 1853 Robert Hickson began iron ship-building, only to be bought out five years later by his manager, Edward Harland. The island was gradually linked to the mainland of Ballymacarrett, and Harland & Wolff started its operations there in 1861.

The recent Odyssey centre - opened in November 2000 with a performance from James Galway, who learned much of his musical skills in the 39th Old Boys Flute Band of East Belfast - reflects the original 'pleasure-dome' character of the district. Even the seating colour - blue - recalls the interior shade of the original palace. Recent praise of the disciplined fans of the Belfast Giants ice-hockey team echoes the 1850s' press reports that everyone was on his or her best behaviour; the only damage recorded to plant life was to a tobacco plant "which presented to juvenile curiosity the temptation ... of ascertaining the flavour of that popular weed". How little has changed!

View of East Belfast

MARTIN D COOKE
UWS.

The quality of housing built for the huge influx of workers into Ballymacarrett from the middle of the 19th century was in dismal contrast to the mansions that the businessmen and entrepreneurs created for themselves.

One of the main areas for terraced housing was the parallel streets which appeared at the lower end of the Newtownards Road, which had been originally termed Ballymacarrett Road. McMaster Street (named after its builder), opposite St Patrick's Church, was built during the last decade of the 19th century, by which stage housing and planning regulations endeavoured to ensure a better standard of working class accommodation.

Whilst the front door may still have opened on to the street, the houses were required to have a rear entrance, with a back yard which had a toilet. Proper communal sewerage had become essential, and water and gas were also piped in. Electricity did not become common-place until at least the 1930s, and the lamp-lighter and window-tapper remained regular visitors up to that time.

The residents of McMaster Street, like all in the area, suffered from the same hardships and deprivation of all their neighbours during the inter-War years. Rev John Redmond at St Patrick's recalled the building of three Mission Halls in the district, and Rev Robert Gallagher later recorded that, when he arrived at the Newtownards Road Methodist Church in 1927: "Not only were the pews empty, but so also were the great gantries in the shipyards and grass was growing where busy feet used to tread, and as most of our men were shipyard workers the prospect was bleak indeed".

The street survived the bombing of the Luftwaffe, which visited so much damage further up the Newtownards Road close to the Arches. In recent years the yellow brickwork of its windows, and other features, have become the target for the conservation programme of the Hearth Housing Association, which is restoring these examples of good 19th century working class housing for letting in the 21st century.

McMaster Street

Newtownards Road

The Head Office of the Ulster Bank was opened in 1836 in Waring Street (on the site of the current War Memorial Building).

The attractive Mountpottinger Branch, established in 1898 on the Albertbridge Road, was designed by J W Blackwood, son of one of the Bank's Directors, J T Blackwood. In the 1970s it briefly became the data processing department of the Ulster Bank before being amalgamated after 100 years of service in 1998 with the neighbouring Connswater branch (which had opened in 1918).

The Paste Room at Head Office was run for many years into the early part of the 20th century by William Porter. The work involved sorting and despatching, and taking remittances to other branches. Any young runner who incurred Porter's displeasure was usually sent on foot to Mountpottinger, the most distant branch in Belfast!

Regulations governing employment in banks - even up to the start of the Second World War - were remarkably imperious. Any officials under the age of thirty had to obtain the approval of the Directors before being permitted to marry, and they could be asked if their fiancée had private means to supplement the salary "to enable you to live in a manner befitting your position as an officer of the Bank". Even up to 1939 the social standing of one's intended was regarded as important!

Women were not employed in the Ulster Bank until the shortage of men began to bite in 1915. Five female clerks were initially employed, a total which rose to 200 until female recruitment was suspended in 1919. Women had to resign if they wished to marry.

One of the ironies of the early Ulster Bank is that they could accommodate the Irishman who went into a bank to change a £9 note because, in addition to the more customary denominations, they printed bank-notes for 25s [£1.25], 30s [£1.50], £2 and £3.

Ulster Bank

Belmont Presbyterian Church (accompanied by a manse and school) was opened for worship on 26 January 1862. It was financed, and the land given, by (the later Sir) Thomas McClure who lived at Belmont House (the site of which is currently occupied by the front quadrangle of Campbell College). Whilst it was an undoubtedly generous act, McClure could well afford it, for - in addition to considerable business investments - he owned a wide swathe of property stretching all the way from the Belmont estate down to Belfast Lough.

In its first one hundred years Belmont Church had only four ministers, perhaps the most notable being the 1903 Moderator of the General Assembly, the Very Rev Dr John MacDermott, father of a future Lord Chief Justice of Northern Ireland. The minister was once rescued from drowning in Ballycastle harbour by Sir Roger Casement. He was apt to preach for over an hour without a scripted sermon, but was known for his integrity and determined principles. As a Governor at nearby Campbell College, he proved vitriolic towards the Headmaster, R A H MacFarland, who during World War I allowed boarders to plant potatoes in the school grounds on the Sabbath.

MacDermott's three sons all joined the Ulster Volunteer Force in 1913, and the youngest - Robin - interrupted his medical career to enlist in 8th (East Belfast) Battalion of the Royal Irish Rifles. He had the misfortune, on 8 January 1916, to become the first officer of 36th (Ulster) Division to be killed.

The Church formed an active Boys' Brigade company in 1892, led with distinction between 1907 and 1913 by the brothers, William and James McKee. The former served in Dublin against the Easter Rising, but was killed in action during the First World War and is commemorated on the celebrated Menin Gate at Ypres (now Ieper).

The younger brother survived the War - but only just; as a Captain in the Royal Irish Rifles he won the DSO and Croix de Guerre, but during the attack on Messines Ridge in June 1917 lost a leg - a tragic blow for someone who had (in common with brother William) played both football and cricket for Cliftonville. In 1925 James became the first Headmaster's secretary at Campbell College, in an age when secretaries were men.

James Craig, the first Prime Minister of Northern Ireland, was baptised in Belmont Church, and his funeral in 1940 was also held here. The coffin was placed on a gun-carriage, drawn by an armoured car, and followed by a procession which wound its way along Massey Avenue to the final resting-place at Stormont.

Belmont Presbyterian Church

SYDENHAM AVENUE

MARTIN D. COOKE
UWS

Glenmachan, like so many late 19th century villas in the Belmont district, was designed by the architect Thomas Jackson, who first built and occupied the nearby Altona. At the end of that century Glenmachan was in the hands of the linen magnate, Sir William Quartus Ewart, whom C S Lewis knew as 'cousin Quartus'. The pious and charitable industrialist offered his young relation a standing invitation to tea, and in later life the author reflected that half-a-mile down the road from Little Lea "Life was more spacious and considered than with us, and glided like a barge where ours bumped like a cart".

C S Lewis would still recognise these modernised cottages, perhaps 150 years old, which are believed to have been cottages for gardeners at Glenmachan. Not inappropriately, it was in this district that, in 1907, Charles Black (a neighbour of the Lewis family at Ardnagreena on the Circular Road) founded the Strandtown Cottagers' Garden Association. This was the first scheme in Ireland to offer urban dwellers a chance to produce their own crops, particularly vegetables and flowers.

There were strict rules for those leasing plots (of approximately 400 square yards), which included preserving the sanctity of the Sabbath, but by 1912 the Association managed 400 plots covering 45 acres. The project developed in popularity; during the war allotments were created, for instance, opposite McCaw, Stevenson & Orr's mill (Loopbridge Mill) and on the site of the current Euston Street - both off the Castlereagh Road - and later at Victoria Road in Sydenham.

By coincidence, Arthur Moore, one of the first pupils in 1894 at the nearby Campbell College, was to become secretary of the related Co-operative Small Holdings Society in England in 1906. The position was not always as sedate as it might appear. Meetings were apt to be disrupted by suffragettes, and on one occasion he had to appear in court when he was charged - wrongly, as it transpired - with manhandling a woman who wanted to address the directors of the Society within hand-bag distance.

Old Cottages
OLD HOLYWOOD ROAD

The Cregagh district between Bellsbridge and the Upper Knockbreda Road (now the Ring Road) was not developed residentially until after the First World War.

Lloyd George, the Prime Minister, had promised "homes fit for heroes to live in", and approximately 150 houses were built for ex-servicemen in this district in the latter half of the 1920s. The streets were to boast names that some of the occupants may have preferred to forget - Bapaume, Picardy, Albert, Somme and Thiepval - battles and towns in France which had demanded a huge sacrifice from the 36th (Ulster) Division. It is one of the very few estates in the United Kingdom which boasts its own granite war memorial, dedicated by the visiting Prince of Wales in November 1932.

The graphic experience of such as the Somme bred a harmonious, communal spirit which helped many through the gloomy inter-War years. Mr Somerville, a one-armed coalman, was ready to oblige customers by supplying coal by stone weight if family resources could not stretch to the price of a full bag.

St Finnian's Church was built to serve this community on what was claimed to be "probably the finest site occupied by any church in Belfast". Its construction required a great act of faith, accompanied by strenuous and dedicated fund-raising, but the foundation stone was laid on 19 September 1931 on land leased from (and eventually donated by) the Marquis of Downshire. Built from Ballycullen stone from the Scrabo quarries, the church, boasting an octagonal baptistery, opened one year later.

One of the leading figures of the St Finnian's congregation was Newton Anderson, who lived adjacently on Downshire Road. He was private secretary to James Craig at Craigavon, and quartermaster to the 36th (Ulster) Division in the first year of World War I, before enlisting in the Royal Irish Rifles. In 1921 he became Permanent Secretary to the Northern Ireland Supreme Court of Judicature.

In the 1930s at 6 Picardy Avenue lived George Dixon, a watchmaker (who was perhaps associated with J Dixon & Co at 51 Ormeau Road). Even from the late 18th century there were numerous watchmakers in the north of Ireland. The essential contribution of Ballymacarrett to the watch industry was the manufacture of watch glass, which was reputedly amongst the best in the world. One of the most noted watch glass makers of the mid 19th century was John Wheeler, who was one of the five listed in the 1850 Belfast Street Directory who were based in Ballymacarrett.

St Finnian's Church
CREGAGH

MARTIN O COOKE
DWS

In the first Ordnance Survey map of the Ballyhanwood district in 1834 the locality is littered with farms and quarries. One of the families which resided in the district for a lengthy period was that of the Shanks, who are recorded as owning or leasing land in the area from the end of the 18th century. They were still there in the early 20th century when the death is recorded in 1910 of Adam Henry Shanks, who had married Miss Stitt, daughter of the Ballyhanwood hearthmoney collector.

One of the leases granted to the Shanks family in the late 18th century was given by Cortland McGregor Skinner, who was associated with the Belfast police service from the 1790s until at least the 1830s. Skinner retired as Superintendent Magistrate of Police in 1833, because of advanced age, but had still been lively enough to arrest a mentally disturbed man who had hacked his own father to death in Smithfield during the previous year.

However, the farming community par excellence of the Ballyhanwood and Gilnahirk districts is the Morrow family, who have farmed the land in the area since at least 1730. The are currently Morrows occupying seven consecutive houses along the road in the accompanying picture!

At the start of the 20th century the Morrows were engaged in bloodstock rearing and training, and racing at such courses as Newmarket, and may be descendants of David Morrow who was agent for Francis Savage's Ballyhackamore racecourse at the end of the 18th century.

The Morrows farm the Hill House Dairy Farm on the slopes of Ballyhanwood, but when they started to sell soft fruit they altered the name to Streamvale. At the end of the 1980s they initiated the Streamvale Open Farm venture.

They remain well-respected members of the local Gilnahirk community. Many of the 19th century elementary schools were run by the local church and, consequently, had their Governors selected by the Church. However, at the current Gilnahirk Primary School four out of the eight appointees are still nominated by the Morrow family!

Tom Morrow of Loughview farm on the road died in 1916 at the age of 102. When he walked down to Hill House Farm on his 100th birthday he was asked how he felt at the start of his second century; "Much stronger than at the start of the first century", he replied. There was considerable humour at the fact that his sons were expected to take the farm into harness - in their 70s!

Ballyhanwood Road

NEAR GILNAHIRK

Leathem Cottage may well be the oldest occupied home in Belfast. It was built, according to its mis-spelled plaque, *Anno Domoni 1786* by Robert Leathem, who died aged 52 on 8 November 1813 after a painful illness. He may not have been greatly missed by some of his neighbours!

At the end of the 18th century, Presbyterians - like Catholics - still suffered from civil and political disabilities. Although they composed the largest denomination in Belfast, and were the primary merchants and traders, generating much of the wealth, they were still precluded from any control of their municipal government.

It was, therefore, no surprise that Belfast Presbyterians were at the forefront of the Volunteer movement founded in the late 1770s which, as Dr A T Q Stewart has written, "turned their attention to politics, becoming an alternative form of popular representation". The establishment of Belfast Royal Academy - which opened in the same year as Leathem built his cottage - was also a feature of growing Presbyterian frustration.

Belfast during the 1780s was to become the centre of severe denominational tension, which spread to the surrounding districts. Robert Leathem, who according to legend used stone from the adjacent Con O'Neill's castle to construct his cottage, built it about one hundred yards from Castlereagh Presbyterian Church (built in 1720).

The use of spies, informants and agents-provocateur by the British authorities was common-place during these times. It may be that Leathem acted in this capacity but, if so, he was not particularly successful.

The minister to the neighbouring Presbyterians, from 1774 to 1806, was Rev Alexander Henry. As a result of an affadavit from Leathem, Henry was tried in mid April 1794 at Downpatrick Assizes for "uttering seditious words against the King and his Government in private conversation". However, no witnesses could be produced, and Henry was "honourably acquitted".

Relationships thereafter must have proved rather tense along Church Road. What the truth was is difficult to determine, but the author of the history of Castlereagh Presbyterian Church wrote: "While Mr Henry was the minister at Castlereagh, both the Presbyterian Church and the country passed through very trying days. Amid the turmoil he seems to have devoted himself to the spiritual good of the people committed to his ministerial care". The Fasti of the Presbyterian Church offers the singular statement that Henry was "a wise teacher of Christianity and an honest man".

Leathem Cottage
CHURCH ROAD, CASTLEREAGH

James Craig senior was born and raised in Ballyvester, the townland adjacent to where this book is published, but eventually moved to Sydenham in East Belfast. He became a millionaire by the age of 50, primarily as a result of his business interests in the Dunville Distillery.

James Craig junior - the future first Prime Minister of Northern Ireland - was born in Sydenham on 8 January 1871, but moved at a very young age to the newly-built family home on the Circular Road at Belmont. Craigavon, set in 35 acres of land, was designed - like so many other villas in the district - by the architect Thomas Jackson.

On the death of his father in April 1900, the young James became the effective owner of the house, which, as Craig's biographer, St John Ervine (born in Isthmus Street off the Woodstock Road), wrote was where "many eventful acts were performed, and much that was important to his country was said and done".

Craigavon was at the epicentre of the tense events during the years of the Ulster Crisis (1911-14), and was to be effectively besieged from 21 March 1914 by military forces endeavouring to prevent the creation of a provisional government by Unionists. The latter held their Cabinet meetings in the large billiard room of the house. The house was also the nerve centre of the secret arms committee which organised the gun-running at Larne on 24 April 1914.

50,000 Ulstermen had massed in the natural amphitheatre of the lawns of Craigavon on 23 September 1911 to listen to Sir Edward Carson rail against the Third Home Rule Bill, and it was here that the Ulster Volunteer Force was conceived and inaugurated on the Twelfth of 1913. Drilling for East Belfast units took place at nearby Ormiston on Hawthornden Road.

During the First World War Craigavon was loaned as a hospital for recuperating soldiers. The Craig family was never to live there again, primarily because when Craig became Prime Minister he was to occupy the official residence at Stormont. Craigavon was sold just after the war for £25,000 to Down County Council as a sanatorium for ex-servicemen, a role which - through the building of additional hospital buildings - it has continued to fulfil.

In recent years it has been occupied by the Somme Association which runs the Somme Heritage Centre at Conlig.

Craigavor
BELMON'

Willowfield Parish Church was built close to Gooseberry Corner and Jocelyn Cottage on what was then the Cregagh Road, but is now part of the Woodstock Road. It was intended to alleviate what one of the Ewart linen family described as "the want of church accommodation and the spiritual destitution of many members of the Established Church in Belfast".

The land for the new church at the junction with My Lady's Road - so called because the route was used by the Marchioness of Donegall when she rode out from Ormeau House - was given in 1868 by William Mullan, mayor of Belfast in 1866, who lived at Willowfield House. In those days the open countryside still stretched back to this villa - on a site behind the current RUC station - and it was clearly visible from the church. Further donations were made by William Coates of Glentoran, John B Houston of Orangefield, Lord Templemore and William Ewart of Glenmachan, who also presented the organ.

Following the consecration of the church in August 1872, a day school was established in 1884. However, the schools' inspector disapproved of "a mixed school so largely attended by boys being conducted solely by [two] female teachers", and the lady principal - 21 year old Miss Elizabeth McDonald - resigned shortly after the school opened. Willowfield No.1 School, as it became named, was closed in 1927, and was transformed into the Parochial Hall; it survives as a doctor's surgery.

Willowfield No.2 School commenced classes in April 1913 further up the Cregagh Road, opposite Daddy Winker's Lane. In 1922 it acquired the name which it bears today - Harding Memorial School - in tribute to Canon Charles William Harding, incumbent at Willowfield from 1900 until his death in 1922.

Despite the fact that German bombs fell close to the church in 1941 - as at Hatton Drive - it survived unscarred, but the original spire which Willowfield boasted proved to be its own worst enemy. It had to be repaired as early as 1884, and in 1912 was removed. It was raised again in 1926, but the attractive green oxidised steeple became unsafe and had to be taken down in 1951.

One hundred parishioners gave their life during the First World War and in 1923 a new organ was inaugurated as an unusual memorial to those who did not return from the battlefields - men such as Alfred William Ground of Newry Street and William Nixon of Woodstock Road, both in the Royal Irish Fusiliers, and J Wardlow of the Seaforth Highlanders from Henryville Street. The current organist, John Gibson Lyttle, has played at the console for forty years.

Willowfield Parish Church

WOODSTOCK ROAD

The district still known familiarly as The Arches, at the junction of the Holywood and Newtownards Roads, derives its name from the former arches of the Belfast & County Down Railway (BCDR) line which ran across this point. The chief engineer of the railway in the mid 1840's was William Dargan, who had been responsible a few years previously for cutting the first channel of the Lagan estuary, which opened up the Belfast docks.

The very unattractive arches - built from Scrabo stone - carried the railway line for exactly one hundred years, from the first rail journey to Comber on 6 May 1850, until they were demolished three years after the final run on 22 April 1950.

The BCDR suffered two major accidents on the line close by at Ballymacarrett Junction. The second of these was on the dark, foggy morning of 10 January 1945, when 23 passengers were killed, and 41 injured.

The first accident occurred on Saturday 13 May when a fireman of the BCDR ran his goods engine off a siding, which was then hit by the passenger train arriving from Donaghadee and Newtownards. In addition to over thirty people being injured, two young passengers lost their lives - a young student from Ballymoney, and a 13 year old daughter of John Bailey, who was the principal book-keeper at Harland & Wolff.

The seriousness of some of the injuries can be gauged from the fact that a number of those injured received compensation ranging from £250 to £1000 - a substantial sum of money in those days. One of those injured was William Booth Pearsall, a Dublin dentist who became a noted sketcher and watercolourist, who later exhibited nearly 500 sketches in Dublin over the years. He received £650, and his wide-ranging travels may well have been financed by this compensation.

The guard of the passenger train, Thomas Wilson, survived the accident, despite his van being "shattered to atoms". He was awarded only £20 compensation, and during his final working years in the 1880s was to become station-master at Knock.

The aftermath of the accident was photographed by the young man, Robert Welch, before he began his career as a notable photographer. The fatal collision attracted a very large crowd as the BCDR endeavoured to repair the line. The collision occurred at 8.25 pm on a Saturday - and by Monday morning the trains were running according to the timetable!

Holywood Arches

Whereas many townland names are anglicised from the Irish, Gransha (Irish: *an ghráinseach*) is one of those rare gaelicised words, denoting a grange. Granges were usually supplementary, outlying estates acquired by medieval monasteries to provide additional supplies for the community - probably, in this instance, for the Cistercian establishment at Comber.

Despite the fact that agricultural production is essential to all mankind, farmers and labourers throughout history have often been treated in a disdainful and unrewarded manner. Economic hardship has often proved a spark for discontent and revolution, as with the Land League of Michael Davitt and Charles Parnell. Yet such workers have rarely been shirkers, and it has been written that "When he went to Great Britain [or even further afield] the Irish harvest labourer or navvy was conspicuous for his endurance and hard work". Speaking of the men of the 18th and 19th centuries, John Stevenson concluded: "The life of the Down farmer for 150 years was of the hardest ... The man of North East Down is still a Scotsman and son of the Kirk's upbringing. To many centuries' endurance by his ancestors of the rigour of a cold northern clime, he owes a hardy physical frame".

Many of the problems of farming - which, even in the early 20th century in the north of Ireland, was the largest employer, providing work for one quarter of the population - were the result of the fact that the overwhelming majority of farms were small. In the 18th century farming in Co Down remained little more than a subsistence economy, and consecutive poor harvests could approximate to a famine. Most of those engaged in farming endured harsh and penurious lives.

One of the basic crops, along with oatmeal, was potatoes; they provided an abundant staple diet, and was a good crop for clearing the land. In the troubled years of the 1790s, potato digging became a useful cover for the fomentation and exercise of political agitation - what Dr A T Q Stewart described as "a strange and novel custom".

If any United Irishman was arrested, his neighbours gathered to lift his potatoes. Quite often these groups totalled betwen 500 and 2000 people, and 6000 was not unknown. They were immensely good-humoured, as even Viscount Castlereagh of Mount Stewart was to testify, despite being firmly opposed to them. A contemporary French traveller recorded: "The whole time the work went on men, women and children sang, accompanied by one or other kind of instrument. No-one is allowed at such gatherings to drink any strong liquor, and this certainly requires a great effort in this part of the country ... For the occasion the peasantry had put on their best clothes".

Farmhouse
GRANSHA ROAI

64

MARTIN D COOKE
UWS

In the late 18th century land in the area of the current Stormont - then called Storm Mount - was owned by Samuel Jackson. However, the development of the estate effectively began with the marriage of Samuel's daughter, Esther, to the Rev John Cleland, rector of Newtownards for twenty years until 1809.

The Christian principles of the Gospel were not a prominent feature of Cleland's character, and he made a colossal fortune from dubious activities, including the unsympathetic extortion of rents from the tenants of the Londonderry family, whose agent he was. He was also greatly disliked by his new neighbours at Stormont, and iritated many by closing the Belfast to Donaghadee coach road which traversed his property.

When his son, Samuel Cleland, succeeded the family had built a plain house on the demesne but, by 1848, it had been remodelled in the Scottish Baronial style (like that at neighbouring Ormiston), and clad with Scrabo stone, ultimately becoming known as Stormont Castle. The Cleland family left the estate in 1893, and the house was leased out. It became vacant in the early 1920s just as the new Northern Ireland Government was created. Stormont Castle was purchased by the latter and, between 1922 and 1940, became the official residence of the Prime Minister, Sir James Craig.

The site of the Parliament building was prepared from 1923, and was officially opened on 16 November 1932 by the Prince of Wales, the future Edward VIII. The processional route from the royal yacht (MV Ulster Prince) along the Newtownards Road, was extremely colourful. Pitt Street displayed a reproduction of the royal yacht; Memel Street arch was painted red, white and blue, and Cable Street - appropriately for its name - had flood-lighting during the night. The walls of Sirocco Works, the Holywood Arches and other buildings were festively decorated. The Prince remained remarkably unenthused; whilst acknowledging the crowds, the press recorded that he "maintained a solemn - almost stern - demeanour throughout the entire proceedings".

The central chandelier in Stormont parliament building was originally a gift to Edward VII from Kaiser Wilhelm II (and still sports the imperial eagle), but this did not hinder the Luftwaffe's attempt to bomb the building in May 1941 - when bombs were dropped, probably by mistake, on Campbell College. Consequently the Portland limestone façade of Stormont was camouflaged with a mixture of tar and cow dung. Someone deserves a 'pat on the back' for that idea!

Stormont

Belmont Primary School - originally in the grounds of the Presbyterian Church in Sydenham Avenue - opened in 1863 offering education to local boys and girls. The current building was funded in 1889 by Sir Robert Ferguson, of Sydenham House at Belmont, as a memorial to his wife Mary, and became known as the Ferguson Memorial School. Designed by Vincent Craig, brother of the later Sir James Craig, it opened in 1893.

Miss McBride ran the girls' section, which was housed on the upper floor, for well over 30 years. Mr H A Skillen was the principal at the boys school from 1880 until the 1920s; he was known for the 'Paddy Hat' which he wore, and also employed for imposing discipline!

As the population in the area grew by the early 20th century, so did the number of pupils. In the first year of the school it accommodated 81 boys and girls; when the new premises opened on the Belmont Road in 1892-93 there were 391 pupils on the roll, with an average attendance of 313.

Many of the earliest pupils came from a wide geographical area - Strandtown (which was also the official name for the Belmont area), Ballyhackamore and even Ballymacarrett. Their parents were cabinet-makers, carters, farmers, sea captains, the Ballyhackamore blacksmith, a washerwoman, gardeners, doctors, grocers, jewellers and the station-master at Sydenham. There were also several children of coachmen at the mansions of Glenmachan, Ormiston, Belmont House (where Campbell College now stands), Strandtown House (the site of the Strand cinema) and The Moat (on the Old Holywood Road opposite Glenmachan).

Early subjects taught in the 1860s and 1870s reflected the rote methods of learning that prevailed: arithmetic and tables, reading, writing and penmanship, and geography, usually taught by displayed maps, which inspectors occasionally criticised as grubby and dilapidated. Perhaps more revealing of the attitudes of the day are the subjects which appear under the description of 'Industrial Training': sewing, knitting, embroidery and crochet work.

Inspectors reports were often generalised and reasonably favourable, but occasionally offered a caustic observation, as in 1917 when it was felt that better organisation was needed. It was suggested that infants and First Standards pupils should be taught by one teacher: "there is no reason", concluded the irritated inspector, "why the infants should be treated as the 'fag end' of the school"!

The building fell into disuse in recent years, but was acquired in April 2001 by the Old Belmont School Preservation Trust, which hopes, after restoration, to find a positive use for it in the community.

Belmont Primary School
Belmont Road

By 1835 there were two Methodist churches very close to one another on the Newtownards Road, where the Masonic Hall now stands. In 1880, one of the two ministers expressed the opinion that neither of the churches was suitable to accommodate the growth of Methodism in the district. According to one visiting preacher in 1872, East Belfast appears to have been fertile ground for preachers: "I preached at Ballymacarrett ... The word was with power by the demonstration of the spirit, and the love feast was rich in saving influence ... On the following Tuesday, Wednesday and Thursday evenings, Brother Wilson and I laboured together to great crowds of people, numbering from two to three hundred at a time".

A new site was sought, and on 19 June 1887 one of the two congregations carried out a symbolic march, led by their minister, to their new place of worship at the junction of Albertbridge Road and Templemore Avenue. The remaining church was demolished by the Luftwaffe in April 1941.

It was admitted that the new church was "not super-elegant in the exterior", but it flourished nonetheless. Its second minister, Rev James Harpur (1888-91) was "probably the most successful soul-winner of his day". He crowded the building at every service, and in the evening it was always impossible to gain admission after 6.45 pm". One of the original Trustees was John Kelly of the coal company, described as "a man of spotless probity and honour", whose family was a major stalwart of Methodism in the north of Ireland.

Further down Templemore Avenue - which was the only part of the district successfully developed as a result of Lord Templemore's aspirations - the vacant site next to the library occasionally witnessed, between the Wars, the erection of marquees for gospel campaigns, or visits from fairground owners such as Barry's. The original Carnegie Library was demolished by a bomb in 1941; it had offered a spacious reading room where newspapers could be read - but all the horse racing details and tips were censored by a thick black pen!

In order to avoid the traffic and tram-lines on the Albertbridge Road, Templemore Avenue was used as a route by cattle and sheep farmers, who then turned into Madrid Street en route to the stockyards at the Albert Bridge. Even in the 20th century one family was shocked to see a terrified cow race up their stairs and become jammed on the landing. It is said that they were grateful that they had used linoleum instead of carpet!

At the junction with Castlereagh Street stood The Farmer's Rest public house. Built in the 1870s, it acquired its name in 1890 as a result of the fact that farmers called in to sell their produce. In the 1890s, only seven doors away at No.94 Castlereagh Street, lived the Kelly coal family.

Mountpottinger Methodist Church

ALBERTBRIDGE ROAD

MARTIN D. COOKE
UWS.

The Pride of Lion Hearted People

The Growth of East Belfast

The rising tide of population was also symbolised by the building of schools and churches; within the space of the decade from 1827 Christ's Church (later St Patrick's Church of Ireland), St Matthew's Roman Catholic and 1st Ballymacarrett Presbyterian churches were all built in the district. Even from the late 18th century Benjamin Edwards had been manufacturing and selling household requisites such as pots, pans, griddles, kettles and irons, all of which imply a ready domestic market. One local advantage for the construction of residential, communal and industrial buildings was the availability of bricks. The prevailing clay-slate proved eminently suitable for the making of bricks, and there were several brickfields in East Belfast on both sides of the Albertbridge Road, the Beersbridge and Castlereagh Roads, and in Ballynafeigh. Bricks not used in the construction of Ballymacarrett or its neighbour across the Lagan were used as ballast in ships plying the Atlantic to the West Indies.

Particularly after William Dargan's excavation of the Lagan estuary, the development of port and harbour facilities consolidated the growth of Ballymacarrett; these enabled the import of essential raw materials (such as cotton, iron and coal) and the export of finished manufactured products (such as textiles, engineering and ships). The shipbuilding industry served the accelerating trade with, and transportation to, America and elsewhere in the world.

Land beyond the municipal boundary tended to be cheaper and to enjoy less burdensome building and leasing restrictions. The willingness of the Donegall cadet line to offer leases in perpetuity in Ballymacarrett was advantageous to those seeking long-term industrial and commercial investment. Indeed, Henry Baron Templemore, who inherited the district in 1837, appears to have sought to emulate Yelverton, and during the 1850s planned to drain the Connswater estuary, and create a structured street plan that would include villas and factory sites. Ironically, this was undermined by the cost of reacquiring the perpetual leases he had granted. The only thoroughfare constructed as a result of this vision was Templemore Avenue, and both Francis Ritchie and Victor Coates were to pocket far more substantial sums from their extensive working class housing projects in the Lagan Village area than did Templemore, their lessor!

The potential for both residential - initially gentlemen's homes rather than terraced housing - and commercial development had been recognised from the late 18th century. A notice in the Belfast News Letter on 14 March 1791 advertised the lease of two fields for sale by auction: "The Wind Mill Farm, containing 31 acres at Beersbridge in Ballymacarrett, situate about three-quarters of a mile from Belfast, on the road leading to Castlereagh - to be let in lots for Town Parks or building on long leases ... There are several good situations for gentlemen's housing". When Robert Wilson was letting a house in Ann Street in October 1797, he also offered the tenant the option on "three acres of the plantation at Beersbridge".

1797 - the months leading up to the 1798 Rebellion - was not the most auspicious time to enter into business agreements. In September of that year, the proprietors of the Beersbridge Flour Mills advertised that they were contracting their business "as much as may be until they shall have peace and tranquillity restored, [and] have determined not to grind any wheat for their own account until that period shall arrive". They indicated also that they were willing to sell the mill on moderate terms. However, more promising and prosperous times returned, and in September 1804 Francis Savage offered for sale or lease 40 to 50 acres of his Racecourse at Ballyhackamore: "the land", he boasted, "is at present in high condition, and would be well worth the attention of any person in the Muslin business, being well supplied with spring water, etc".

In spite of the industrial prospect on the Lagan shore at the close of the 18th century, two hundred years ago the whole of East Belfast retained its rural character. Reflecting this was the sale of the lease for a "snug little cabin" (Belfast News Letter, 26 March 1799):

"lately occupied by James Kennedy Trail, situated in Beersbridge within twenty minutes walk of Belfast. On the ground floor there is a parlour, kitchen and two bedchambers; with an abundance of room above stairs for several servants. There is also a ... stable, capable of containing two horses and a cow ... and a neat garden".

The agricultural hallmark of the lower Cregagh (now the Woodstock Road) in the 1830s is apparent in the story in the Belfast News Letter (26 April 1830) which related the misfortune of the farmer, Robert Carlile, who "on the Cregagh Road - only a mile from Belfast" lost his house, farm buildings and associated possessions in a fire - although it was recorded by one of his neighbours that he was also a "road contractor". The Carlile family - many of whom are buried in the graveyard of Castlereagh Presbyterian Church - were still listed as farmers, and continued to live on the Cregagh Road, into the 1870s and 1880s. Indeed at that stage the majority of the residents of Castlereagh were listed as farmers; David Hammond has written that "as late as even 1928 the area was still partly inhabited by dairy farmers who sold milk daily off spring carts in the streets of Belfast". In August 1830 John B Shannon of Laganvale, who owned one of the vitriol works, publicised that he had made the first cut of "a most excellent crop of oats" - grown in Ballymacarrett! Samuel Elliott, a much travelled adventurer, was born on 19 February 1835 on a farm almost on the site of the current Willowfield police station.

Many of the large houses in the Ballymacarrett and lower Ballyhackamore districts - such as Turf Lodge (where Samuel Davidson of Sirocco fame once lived), Henryville House, Glentoran (the home of Victor Coates, originally called Snug Brook) and Shamrock House - boasted productive gardens. However, as industrialisation confirmed its grip, and the Belfast boundary was extended (effectively to the Connswater river) to incorporate the Ballymacarrett

townland in 1854, the merchants and industrialists began to move up the gentle contours to the more salubrious and less congested Strandtown, Knock and Belmont. Much of this district was owned by Sir Thomas McClure, who lived at Belmont House (on the site of the current Campbell College); it was he "who, by forming convenient roads, fences and plantations, and granting long building leases, [gave] a great impetus to the improvements in the district".

The Businesses and Industry

Attendant upon the success of the 18th century industries of glass making and iron production, other ventures proliferated. The manufacture of vitriol - used extensively for bleaching linen - began in earnest in the early 19th century, with the establishments of John B Shannon at Bridge End and William Boyd in the Lagan Village. The Ordnance Survey map of 1834 shows a bleach mill at the top of the Cregagh Road.

The Ordnance Survey Memoirs of the 1830s reveal that "the greater part of the inhabitants [of Ballymacarrett] are employed in weaving muslins, calicoes and all kinds of cotton cloth", the manufacture of which was controlled by Nick Downey, Samuel Weir, Robert Smith and John Young. However, the gravitation towards a factory-based economy was to cause considerable hardship to the domestic economy. By 1850 there were four large spinning mills along the gentle banks of the Connswater.

Accompanying a multiplicity of individual businesses such as those of blacksmith, farrier, wheelwright and boot and shoe manufacturer, were numerous large-scale companies such as Fortescue Gregg's salt works, Ritchie's and Richardson's chemical and fertiliser works, the Ballymacarrett Pottery Works, Webb's and York's Metal Works, James Tedford's chandlery, Kelly's coal importation business, and the felt manufactories of Anderson and Francis Ritchie. In the latter third of the 19th century brewing and distilling made an appearance with the Avoniel and Connswater (or Irish) Distilleries, and McConnell's brewery on the banks of the Lagan opposite Central Station.

Even these came to be dwarfed by the industrial might of engineering, rope-making and shipbuilding. The first major engineering works was that of McClenaghan and Stainton at Short Strand, inherited in 1802 by the hairdresser Victor Coates, which became the Lagan Foundry. By 1848 it was claimed that "no part of England could produce better steam engines" than Coates's business; its machines were installed in hundreds of factories and businesses, and in 1838 Coates became the first person to build an iron ship, named *The Countess of Caledon*.

Other engineering companies in East Belfast included the St Ann's or Musgrave Foundry at Cluan Place, and Ritchie, Hart & Co. The latter produced Samuel Davidson's prototypes until in 1881 he formed his own company, Sirocco, which by 1930 was manufacturing seventy per cent of the world's tea industry machinery. When the First World War broke out in 1914, Sirocco ventilation and other engineering equipment was to be found in the navies of Britain, Germany and America.

Ropemaking, which seems to have owed much to the inspiration of Henry Joy McCracken's father in the late 18th century, had a long tradition in Ballymacarrett, appearing on the Mount Pottinger road in the 1791 Williamson Map. There were a number of such companies, including those of the Hampson brothers and the Lemon family, but these were submerged by the creation in 1875 of the Belfast Ropeworks Company by William Smiles and Gustav Wolff. It became the largest rope manufacturer in the world, with 30,000 global customers at the start of the 20th century.

Shipbuilding laid its foundations on the Co Down bank of the Lagan with Ritchie's yard on Queen's (originally Dargan's) Island, but this was transformed beyond recognition following the formation in 1861 of Harland & Wolff, eventually the largest shipbuilder in the world. There were others, such as Workman, Clark & Co, which in occasional years outstripped the production of its rival.

In the 20th century new industries arrived, such as Short's aircraft manufacture at Sydenham, but the recently-departed century witnessed a dramatic erosion of industrial and manufacturing output in East Belfast, and it is to be hoped that the Greater East Belfast Partnership and East Belfast Business Initiative will succeed in the economic regeneration of a proud district.

The Industrialists and Inventors

The industrial enterpreneurs who had created employment in the district were hard task masters, but were equally demanding of themselves - for instance, Sir Edward Harland,

Viscount Pirrie and his nephew, Thomas Andrews, chief designer of the *Titanic*, all went through lengthy apprenticeships to learn their trade - and it must be conceded that it was they who created the wealth, as was occasionally acknowledged. When East Belfast sought a new parliamentary candidate in 1895, the chairman of the meeting, James McNaught, said that: "They knew that Mr Wolff and his partner, Sir Edward Harland, had been the making of that district ... 36 years ago Ballymacarrett was a wilderness; now it was a large and populous district of the city, inhabited by industrious, loyal and contented people, and this great change had been brought about by the enterprise of Mr Wolff and his partner".

The contemporary press could be deferential and sycophantic to the barons of industry. When Pirrie went to the great shipyard in the sky in 1924, the Belfast News Letter chose to be inordinately reverential: "... his fertile mind, inventive genius, and imaginative power and foresight led

him from one enterprise to another until, eventually, he exercised an authority in the shipbuilding world which caused him to be singled out as one of the most notable industrial pioneers who have ever made their mark upon history. He was a man of big ideas, indomitable courage and perseverance, endowed with a magnetic personality, and complete confidence in himself and in the schemes which were evolved in his marvellous brain"!

However, cynicism aside, the industrialists of East Belfast were typical of their age. Pirrie claimed that 'his richest possession' was a book of maxims collected for him by his mother. These reflected the opinions and traits of inquisitive, successful and self-confident men of the age such as the American Benjamin Franklin, who exhorted men to be industrious, frugal, punctual and adventurous. William Smiles of the Ropeworks was the son of the noted Victorian philosopher, Dr Samuel Smiles, who wrote the enormously influential classic *Self*

Help, which advocated creativity and self-reliance. One of Dr Smiles' inspirations was none other than Edward Harland.

The visionary and adventurous characters of the period were such as David Livingstone, Charles Darwin and Thomas Edison, and many of the leading businessmen and entrepreneurs of East Belfast were to be influenced by them. Thomas Edison died with nearly 1100 patents to his name and, whilst not quite in the same league, Sir Samuel Davidson, the founder of Sirocco Works in 1881 - born into a farming family - totalled over 120 patents. His early inventions were to revolutionise the tea industry, but he eventually diversified into all types of engineering. Davidson's prototype tea machinery had been made by the local firm Ritchie, Hart & Co, and they seem to have been sufficiently versatile to produce any machinery, given the drawings or models from which to work.

Whilst Sir Edward Harland may be

best remembered for the company which bears his name, the contemporary Daily Star said in an obituary at Christmas 1895: "he was not merely a highly competent businessman; he is entitled to take his place amongst the great inventors of the last half-century". The long, narrow ships which he designed were scorned by his Liverpool rivals, but they were to trim at least a week off a trans-Atlantic run. He took out patents for propellor arrangements, and another trade magazine considered that his "greatest achievement was the twin screw, and this made the name of his firm".

Probably the most consistently versatile company of East Belfast was the Lagan Foundry of Victor Coates, who proved a true pioneer of the engineering trade. One historian has written of the company: "They started by making pots and pans, bleachers' equipment, and barkmills; their main activity became the making of steam engines and boilers, but they also built iron ships ... they made equipment for many local industries, including paper making, flour milling, distilling and soap-boiling; a large part of their business was structural work such as cranes, bridges and metal chimneys ... [yet] they were prepared to undertake repairs and jobbing work, and at one time acted as general iron-founders". The original Victor Coates began in the 1780s effectively as an agent for the company of McClenaghan and Stainton in the Lagan Village. He fortuitously inherited the company in 1802 - but his original career was as a hairdresser in Castle Street!

Whilst the ambition and creative drive of the district was perhaps most celebrated through the more well-known entrepreneurs, the instinct was evident in many of the smaller businessmen of East Belfast. Alexander Mitchell, despite being virtually blind from the age of 22, established a brick-making and building trade, and invented the Mitchell screw-pile (patented in 1833), which enabled the siting of lighthouses in mud-banks and shifting sands as at Holywood in 1844 (as well as at other UK and American locations).

In the 1860s Thomas McDowell founded the Mountpottinger Drug Hall, originally established on the Albertbridge Road, but which eventually moved to larger premises on the Mountpottinger Road. According to one source: "he is the inventor of several special preparations and remedies which command an extensive sale". One of his successors in this market was Horatio Todd, (whose shop is still on the Holywood Road,) who created his own perfumes and linctuses, which he even sold to royalty and the aristocracy.

One of the most famous and successful names in Northern Ireland's retailing trade developed his business from East Belfast. J L Stewart opened the first of his numerous Cash Stores in September 1911 at 334 Beersbridge Road. He developed a flair for knowing the better side of the street, and aimed to sell the best quality goods at the keenest price. He paid for his goods in cash, and accepted only cash from his customers. Even when the company was purchased in the 1930s by Weston's it retained its familiar name, which survived until the take-over by Tesco's in the 1990s.

Reflecting the subtle counterpoint that exists in history, whilst the destructive rioting still flared on the Newtownards Road and Short Strand in the early days of 1922, a young inventive and inspired 14 year old was starting school in East Belfast. A few months later the young Eric Megaw defied the school regulations of Campbell College and built himself a crystal radio set using his dormitory bed-frame as an aerial. One night he became the first person in Ireland to pick up a radio message from New Zealand. From that seminal moment, Megaw went on professionally to conduct important maritime radio experiments, and it was his practical development of the cavity magnetron, so critical to the success of radar, which resulted in the loss of 173 German bombers over England in early 1941

which persuaded Hitler to drop his plans for the sea-borne invasion of England.

Pleasant Surroundings

Ballymacarrett became submerged by factories and rows of terraced houses built by such men as Ritchie and Coates to accommodate their employees. The latter family, by the early 20th century, built and owned thirty-three streets, principally between the current Ravenhill and Woodstock Roads. A century earlier the quality of working class housing was particularly squalid. Some improvements were made in the 1840s and 1870s as a result of various bye-laws, but individuals such as the artist Rowel Friers could still recall in the early 20th century the typical single-storey whitewashed cottages, of which "a tall man could have touched the guttering should he have felt so inclined".

Virtually all the houses built after 1857 were still standing a century later when Ernest Jones compiled his *Social*

Geography of Belfast. Victor Coates's residence, Glentoran, in the lower Ravenhill area, was replaced at the very start of the 20th century by kitchen and parlour houses in Dunvegan, Ballarat and Bendigo Streets. By that stage, the whole of inner East Belfast had submitted to the terrace, and only The Mount - the original focus of the district - even then starting to fade, reflected the more prosperous years of Ballymacarrett.

The Working Man

As the commercial development of the 19th century gathered relentless momentum many from Belfast's rural hinterland sought the security of regular employment in the towns. As one observer has commented: "Many of the people who lived [in East Belfast] were rural - the sons and daughters of farming people from North Down or the Lagan Valley" - but it is hard to concede that their quality of life had improved. The inhabitants of the district have, as David Hammond - a local historian and resident - has emphasised, endured "depressions, wars, sectarian conflicts and the toil and tyranny of the job" - and that is in the last century alone. Disease, bad housing, crime and other antisocial behaviour have also been attendant problems.

The working man was the lubricant and life-blood of East Belfast's economic prosperity, as an obituary on the founder of the Belfast Ropeworks Company, William Smiles (who died on 9 January 1904), conceded: "as no-one would have more readily admitted than himself, the efforts of such leaders [of industry] would have been completely useless without the skill and perseverance of their hard-working work-people".

Although many of these men - and women, particularly at such establishments as the Ropeworks - generated considerable wealth for their employers, few of them prospered themselves. The legend flourished that even on his death-bed Lord Pirrie, chairman of Harland & Wolff, asked

for his sword: When asked why, he said: "I want to take another cut at the wages before I go"!

Recording the reflections of those employed at Queen's Island, David Hammond has shown that, as well as being impoverished, the working man's life was often irksome, perilous and discomfitting. It was lore at the shipyard that "there are no old welders, that no welders retire ... the welding is not a very healthy job". Samuel Elliott born in February 1835, on what is now the Woodstock Road, recalled losing one finger and lacerating the other four as the result of an encounter with a circular saw at Victor Coates's Lagan Foundry - and probably regarded himself as fortunate.

At least a dozen men died as a result of the collapse, on 11 January 1851, of a new flax preparation mill under construction, adjacent to the Owen O'Cork mill, at Beersbridge. One of the causes of the fatal accident appears to have been - in order to save money on the contract - the deliberate mixing

of old bricks with new ones. There was an attempt to prosecute Mr Boyd, the owner, and James Magee, the contractor, for manslaughter. Ultimately in a sample case, it was determined that the unfortunate labourer, James Watson, had died "accidentally, casually and by misfortune".

Less than half a mile away, 32 years later, almost to the day (9 January 1883), John Quinliven, stationmaster at Bloomfield, was killed by a train at the crossing gates which were used to span the Beersbridge Road. Because the inquest asserted that Quinliven (who was only 30 years old) had been given too much responsibility, his employers - the Belfast & County Down Railway - were shamed into offering his wife and children a gratuity of £75. Such financial consolation was rare amongst the industrial book-keeping of East Belfast businesses; as David Hammond has shown, most victims of industrial accidents were usually intimidated and threatened out of injury compensation (fatal or otherwise). Indeed, for many of the inhabitants of East Belfast, the only compensations appear to have been the good humour and neighbourliness generated by one's association with the area.

Very few of the inhabitants of East Belfast are known by name until the start of the 19th century. The Raven Maps of 1625 imply an almost non-existent population, yet it is hard to believe that, with all the contractual "appurtenances" which William Kelso could exploit twenty years later, there was not a growing number of tenants and tax-payers. Some of their neighbours included the Beer(e) family - a number of whom are buried in the old Knock graveyard - who were to give their name to Beersbridge.

The latter is one of those locations in East Belfast (in company with such as Bloomfield and Strandtown) which echo its flourishing anglicisation. However, all the townland names (such as Ballymacarrett, Ballyhackamore, Cregagh, Carnamuck and Castlereagh)

are all derived from the original Gaelic. Until the early 19th century, as with Con O'Neill, the native inhabitants spoke Irish. However, with East Belfast's maritime location, its proximity to Scotland, and the arrival of settlers from across the Irish Sea under those with Scottish connections (such as Hugh Montgomery and William Kelso), the language was transformed. Lieutenant Bordes, clerk to the Ordnance Survey Memoirs in 1832, noted that the inhabitants of Ballymacarrett "are half Scotch in their language and manners", and Mr and Mrs Hall, during their tour of Ireland a decade later, stated that in the North Down region "mongrel Scotch is spoken".

The major influx of residents began with the introduction of the factories in the final score years of the 18th century. Bordes commented that in 1832 the "principal occupation is agriculture", but that native Ballymacarrett traveller, Samuel Elliott (born in the same decade), elaborated: "I may here remark that muslin hand-

loom weaving in those days was a remunerative employment, and was indulged in by most of the farming class during the winter season".

The Ordnance Survey Memoirs divulge that: "the greater part of the inhabitants are employed in weaving muslins, calicoes and all kinds of cotton cloth. There are no muslin manufactories of any weight or capital in Ballymacarrett". Most of these men were engaged by manufacturers based across the Lagan. Bordes intimated that the income of these domestic weavers in 1832 was variable but viable.

The 1852 Street Directory suggests that hand-loom weaving was still widely practised in the district, but the reality is that, by that stage, it had become an increasingly fragile employer. Elliott recalled Samuel McMurran's small provision shop which was "principally a tick shop for weavers who frequented it very much, running up large scores in bad times, at very high prices, which they wiped out with the return of better days". Pawnbroking became a more common and very lucrative business - in 1850 one pawnbroker lived at Portview, the house which gave its name to the present commercial complex on the Newtownards Road - and by 1880 there were over 100 pawnbrokers in Belfast, which by that date had encompassed the limits of Ballymacarrett.

The population of East Belfast increased noticeably during the second quarter of the 19th century, the Belfast News Letter proving inclined, whenever it referred to Ballymacarrett, to describe it as "an extensively and densely populated district" (or in similar vein). The Ordnance Survey Memoirs state that in 1821 the townland played host to fewer than 3000 inhabitants; by 1832 this had risen to 5168 accommodated in 791 houses. Elsewhere, in the parish of Knockbreda there were 3900 locals occupying 720 homes. By the middle of the century Samuel Lewis indentified 10627 residents in the

latter, with Ballymacarrett's population having risen to 6697 in 1124 houses. Perhaps surprisingly, Ballyhackamore had only 126 occupants.

Poverty

Daily living standards for most of these people were woefully austere and pitiable during the 1830s and 1840s. In February 1830, the curate of the recently formed parish of Ballymacarrett (from the once extensive Knockbreda), Rev John Henry Potts, gave a charity sermon for "the relief of the poor weavers of Ballymacarrett, whose condition had reached the very extreme of destitution". He estimated that these totalled at least 150 families (with five members per family) out of a population of 5000 (15% of the community).

He pronounced that sickness, exacerbated by the cold weather, "and the want of even ordinary necessities of life, is widely prevalent amongst the poor ... The state of destitution and

wretchedness to which numbers amongst the working class of our population have been reduced by absolute poverty is inconceivable to those who have not witnessed it".

Potts explained that many depended upon their loom for subsistence, but the trade had recently stagnated: "A weaver, who rises to his work at 4 o'clock in the morning, who labours with little intermission until near midnight, cannot earn more than 4s 6d [23p] per week; from this sum deduct 1s [5p] for rent, for coals 6d [2.5p], candles 6d - leaving any provision for the purchase of clothing out of the question - and the remainder is 2s 6d [13p] profit each week. But, in three cases out of four, the poor weaver has a family to support on this miserable pittance of 2s 6d. Nor is he even certain of that small return, for, owing to the glutted state of the market, he cannot at times obtain any employment, and so his scanty earnings are wholly suspended".

At a subsequent meeting, held in

Ballymcarrett parish church (originally called Christ's Church, now St Patrick's on the Newtownards Road), chaired by the Marquis of Donegall, many donations were offered which, within three days, were reported to have totalled £170. John Kane of Turf Lodge donated £3, as did John Shannon of the vitriol works and Mr J Montgomery of Beersbridge. The Blakistons and Houstons who lived at Orangefield also sent a donation. Others from beyond the boundaries of East Belfast demonstrated concern. Francis Turnley of Rockport gave £5; Narcissus Batt of Purdysburn, who had business interests in the area, doubled that sum, as did the Marquis whose family were closely associated with the townland. However, perhaps more significantly, revealing the disparity that often exists in close proximity, the largest sum - £13 2s [£13.10] - was collected by the workmen of the Coates and Young foundry; even the employees at the distant Killyleagh cotton mills sent £5.

Urgent assistance was offered to 72 families, but Potts realised that local people had their pride - a constant feature of the district - and were averse to accepting support perceived as being unconcealed charity. The principle of the scheme was to sponsor local shops who could then sell necessities at greatly reduced prices. Also, although it could have achieved only limited success, it had become common practice for judicial fines to be distributed for the purposes of poor relief. For instance, the local minister, Rev Charles Courtenay, received £2 7s 3d [£2.36] from fines levied in Belfast during July 1835, and also just before Christmas of the same year a seasonal 18s 4d [92p], a fine paid by Samuel Houston and Joseph Purse "for furious and improper driving".

In October 1835 the church was the venue for yet a further charity sermon, "for the purpose of providing comfortable winter clothing for the most destitute families in that populous but indigent district". The minister endeavoured to play upon the consciences of the businessmen across the Lagan; as the municipal boundary stopped at the river, the districts of East Belfast received no support from the town but, as was pointed out, many of those living in Ballymacarrett crossed the bridge to work as "the mechanics and artisans of the merchants of Belfast".

There appears to have been a reluctance on the part of many weavers to recognise the changing times, and the recession occasioned in the late 1840s by the Great Famine assaulted the hand-loom weavers of Ballymacarrett very badly indeed. Official reports indicated that the three worst affected areas in Co Down were the Mournes, Rathfriland - and Ballymacarrett! The latter was equated with one of the worst affected areas in the whole of Ireland - Skibbereen in Co Cork - and a local relief committee had to be established.

Even in better times, the daily diet for many people cannot have been appetising. Writing in the 1880s, Samuel Elliott mentioned that vitriol and starch factories in the area had stopped production: "The void caused by the disappearance of the starch works, must have been, for a time, felt by the poor man's family, the members of which, in many a household, as well as the pigs they reared, being almost wholly fed from the starch washings, a fluid called sowans, which when boiled became a stout paste or porridge, which, with new milk, was very much relished as a meal by the poorer class of people". However by that stage of the century Elliott believed that in East Belfast "the whole tenor of its present state speaks of a far more comfortable and prosperous state of affairs than existed in the [olden] days".

The wheel of fortune continued to revolve, however, and Rev Robert Gallagher later recalled that, when he arrived at the Newtownards Road Methodist Church in 1927, the inter-War years were taking their toll: "Not only were the pews empty, but so also were the great gantries in the shipyards and grass was growing where busy feet used to tread, and as most of our men were shipyard workers the prospect was bleak indeed".

Living Conditions

The industrial, terraced kitchen-style house flourished in the second half of the 19th century and became ubiquitous. By 1901 the only area of East Belfast which reflected the area's erstwhile residential prosperity was The Mount; most of the former villas had been flattened and built over. The dividing line tended to be the fifty foot contour close to The Arches; beyond that point the grimness of residence and cacophony of industry began to recede.

When Francis Ritchie and Victor Coates commenced the industrialisation of the Lagan Village, whitewashed rows of houses were built in places such as Short Strand, Lennon's Row, Bridge End and Gooseberry Corner. These were usually of very poor quality, and those at the latter location (at the junction of the Woodstock and Beersbridge Roads), built as late as the 1860s, were notorious. One of the principal problems of the area was damp. Many homes at the Lagan Village and Bridge End were built on low-lying reclaimed slob-land and, until damp-proof courses were made obligatory in 1899, the floors and walls were susceptible to rising damp and cold, and were apt literally to freeze in winter.

Overcrowding in the small houses was endemic, but the workplaces were equally insalubrious. The 1852 report by Dr A G Malcolm into the sanitary state of the principal establishments concluded that "All of these are characterised by numbers (in many instances amounting to many hundreds) of young persons congregated for many hours daily in a limited space. In some, it is a great object to keep the rooms at a certain, and that a high, temperature. It is plain that, unless the utmost precautions are taken to prevent the accumulation of respired, and therefore vitiated, air the greatest danger to health may be expected".

This was not alleviated by conditions on the public highway. Malcolm's report mentioned that "The chief distinguishing mark of the character of the town, in which I here include the district of Ballymacarrett, is the great want of systematic drainage. No doubt there is some kind of drainage, but it is mostly of a primeval character, signifying that the rain from the clouds and the sewage from the dwellings, are at liberty to make their own intersections and channels, without any interference on the part of man". This is an echo of the 1849 report on Ballymacarrett: "An almost complete want of drainage, extensive accumulations of liquid manure here and there immediately in the rere of the dwelling houses, and a general absence of house accommodation are its chief characteristics. The only regular main sewer, extending from the Holywood Road past the Vitriol Works, and entering the Queen's Quay, though good, effects little improvement in the absence of branch drains".

It was probably difficult to avoid these unpleasant circumstances as the roads themselves were extremely poor. The Ordnance Survey clerk, in 1832, reported that, although some improvements had been made, the roads "are not kept in good repair; even the high road (or mail coach road) to Donaghadee is in a very bad state owing to not having people constantly on them to fill up the holes". In 1847, a correspondent to the Belfast News Letter notified the County Surveyor that "in consequence of the late frost [the Belfast to Holywood road] is completely broken up, and requires instant attention and repairs". Two months later a member of the Grand Jury complained "of the filthy state in which the road through Ballymacarrett was kept. It was a disgrace to the county", he suggested.

It is little wonder that - as early as 1833 - a public dispensary was established for Ballymacarrett to help counter the insalubrious, even pestilential, character of the district, but even that seemed half-hearted.

One of the subscribers to the project complained that unless it had a resident medical practitioner it would prove no more effective than the one in Belfast had been up to that time.

From the mid-1840s various improvement Acts were passed which formulated minimum housing standards. These included facilities such as a window for every room, piped water to every house, no cellars to be used as a dwelling area, and a back yard at least 10 foot square for access. By the 1880s houses such as those being added to Cluan Place (at Mountpottinger) had to boast modern flush toilets. Bye-laws of 1865 and 1878 also laid emphasis upon proper paving and public sewerage.

However, regulation and reality did not always keep in step. It is claimed that by the late 1890s there were still 20,000 out of 70,000 houses (despite the 1878 regulations) which still did not benefit from rear access, and when Ernest Jones wrote his *Social Geography of Belfast* in 1960 "practically all the houses built after 1857 [were] still standing and occupied" - a century later. Domestic gas lighting, which replaced candles and oil, was not common until the end of the 19th century.

Crime

Economic and social hardship are apt to invite attendant evils - and East Belfast proved to be no exception. As early as 1784 the Belfast News Letter published a reward "for the discovery and conviction of trespassers in fields of Ballymacarrett who damaged the grass, destroyed gates and stole the locks, staples and hinges". Horse stealing was common, and presumably a relatively easy crime to commit. As if to demonstrate that some criminals can use or sell almost anything, in November 1815 William Seed and Robert Bailie, the owners of Beersbridge Mills, announced that on a Saturday night "some person or persons did feloniously cut and carry away the sails of our windmill at Beersbridge and, as they are weather-beaten, may easily be detected if applied to any other use, or offered for sale".

Natural and raw materials have always been ready targets. However, all such materials - such as kelp (seaweed) harvested for the purpose of nurturing the soil - usually belonged to the landowner, who expected recompense. John Smylie, one of the glasshouse owners at Short Strand clearly wearied of losing his raw materials, and in June 1791 advertised for two watchmen, and warned that "Any person found raising or carrying away sand, gravel, stones or soil off the Short Strand, or stealing cinders off the bank at the Glasshouse, will be prosecuted as the law directs".

The major employers of the district, perhaps because wages were perceived to be so basic, were the focus for thieves, some of whom were probably employees who regarded such acquisitions as 'perks'. Many of the employees of the Belfast & County Down Railway - booking clerks, goods clerks, ticket collectors and even stationmasters - applied 'creative accountancy' to their books, and many were caught and dismissed. Even one of the Permanent Way Inspectors at Belfast lost his position in February 1882 because he was found to be taking home old sleepers for firewood at his home in Ballygowan.

William Smiles, Managing Director of the Ropeworks, was an insomniac, but he particularly irritated his wife early one morning when he paced the bedroom floor, alleging that he knew something was wrong at the factory. Travelling the mile from his Sydenham home to his Connswater factory, he was just in time - at 4 am - to intercept a lorry load of rope which was being stolen. It became notorious, even in the 20th century, that the home of many a shipyard worker was decorated from the Harland & Wolff stores: linoleum, brass fittings, carpets, wood panelling, doors and paint were all gratefully 'liberated'.

One of the easiest places in

Ballymacarrett to intercept unsuspecting victims - before it was replaced in the 1840s - was the half-mile Long Bridge. In December 1829 a prosecutor called John Mackenzie was unseasonably assaulted there late on Christmas Eve by Hugh McGuigan and some accomplices. Mackenzie had his gun taken and, although able to recover it, was then stabbed. The occasion earned McGuigan a seven year transportation sentence.

Nevertheless, the judicial system could prove fair. Robert Campbell and Samuel McCune were indicted for killing John Smiley on 4 February 1831 in Ballyhackamore. The evidence proved contradictory and confused, and both the defendants obtained excellent character references from the hirsute minister of Castlereagh Presbyterian Church (close to the site of Con O'Neill's castle), Rev Henry Haslett. The latter admitted that Campbell lacked a little self-discipline, but "was a decent young man, [if] at times rather quarrelsome". Haslett's intervention secured their acquittal.

A constabulary office was established in Ballymacarrett in the early 19th century. Occasionally it was successful, as in December 1835, when Sergeant Armstrong identified and arrested "part of a gang of miscreants who lately ... committed nightly depradations". Hugh McGrillias and John Murray were arrested, and stolen property was recovered. On other occasions, as in 1847, the police office was vilified, especially by frustrated farmers: "Here is a large gang of thieves who were accustomed for a number of weeks regularly to pass through Holywood and Ballymacarrett during the night, or early in the morning, laden with plunder, and yet the police who had been made aware of their robberies ... seem to have used no exertions to secure their detection".

To be fair, Armstrong and his colleagues were understaffed. Samuel Elliott claimed that, as a child, he and his friends played shinny (akin to lacrosse) away from the public gaze where they were less likely to come under the scrutiny of the police "which

in those days were few and far between - one sergeant, one corporal and three men having control of Ballymacarrett, Lagan Village, Mountpottinger and the surrounding districts" - and this to serve a population approaching 7000, let alone dealing with external predators. By the mid 19th century the burgeoning district of Ballymacarrett was already gaining a boisterous, even seamy, reputation, and in 1847 the Belfast News Letter referred to it as "that fertile field of shindies and rencontres".

Drink

Much of this was, inevitably, the result of alcohol - some employers were even known to pay their men in the pub! An 1836 survey of Belfast, which included Ballymacarrett, stated that there were 751 outlets selling alcohol. Some of the earliest public houses (pre-1820) were The Glass House and The Windmill and, in Ballyhackamore, The Wheatsheaf. In his final years (the 1880s) Samuel Elliott witnessed the construction of distilleries in East

Belfast, "for the manufacture of the spirit *craythur*, now so much in demand by the working classes". In the early 20th century it was claimed, with little exaggeration, that there was a pub on the corner of nearly every street along the Newtownards Road. Landlords had hundreds of pints already waiting on the counter for the massive human influx after the end of the Friday work shifts, and many of them could sell 1000 pints in the first hour without too much difficulty. There were few pubs, like Holy Joe's (Murray's) at the corner of Cluan Place on the Mountpottinger Road, where the landlord told his customers to go home first after their shift and hand over their housekeeping money.

Some of the establishments became legendary. One pub, near the lower end of the Newtownards Road opposite the Popular cinema, was McKaig's: "However, locals called it the Power Station, and claimed that when one drank of the wine served here ... you entered another world. One old timer [said] that they saw men go in on crutches and walk out without them"!

As Elliott implied, the consumption of alcohol was widespread, and it trespassed frequently upon the workplace. Railway employees often spent their breaks in the local taverns, and alcohol was to blame for the fatal accident at Ballymacarrett Junction in May 1871. The culprit - a fireman on one of the trains involved, who lived on the Ballymacarrett Road (the predecessor to the Newtownards Road) - was not too difficult to find; the last pub he had been in was ten doors up the street from his house, and the constabulary office was a similar distance away towards the Queen's Bridge! The irony was that the police were equally afflicted, and it came to be accepted by the authorities that, if you disciplined every policeman for having a drink on duty, there would be no experienced men in the force!

Alcoholism beset women as much as men. Only a few days after the rail accident sub-constable Farrelly found a married woman of Bread Street (off the Newtownards Road) named O'Neill lying in the road. She was taken to Belfast General Hospital in Frederick Street, where she was found to be suffering from alcohol poisoning, and had to have her stomach pumped. The Belfast News Letter commented rather ruefully: "the frequency of cases of this character is becoming remarkable, a circumstance which cannot fail to be regarded with regret".

One of the principal nurseries of this social affliction was the spirit grocery. Rev John Redmond, the minister at St Patrick's Church, lamented that in the early 1920s there were 54 of these outlets in the side streets of the Newtownards and Albertbridge Roads, and "were constant temptations and snares to my parishioners, especially married women". They were grocery stores which were also off-licences, and many women became enthralled as a result of illegally offered free drinks whilst they were doing their shopping.

John Oliver, who became a

Permanent Secretary at Stormont, was to reflect on his time as a child on the Ormeau Road during these years: "How often was I despatched as a child by a friendly neighbour, Mrs Rafferty, to MacQuillan's shop to buy a quarter pound of tea - and while I was in the shop would I just buy her a glass of whiskey as well?" Redmond listed 82 spirit groceries and 44 pubs in the Mountpottinger sub-district of East Belfast alone, and his crusade resulted in a Licensing Act of the Northern Ireland Parliament wiping them out in 1923 - but not before he had squarely laid quite a lot of the blame for the East Belfast riots of the previous two or three years on the spark of alcohol.

Pastimes

Many of the inhabitants of East Belfast could, nevertheless, handle themselves with dignity and decorum. Samuel Elliott confessed that 19th century children engaged in mischievous - even occasionally malicious - pranks, but the poet W R Rodgers, who lived at Mountpottinger Corner in the early part of the 20th century, recalled that everything ceased for Sundays: "nothing, absolutely nothing, was allowed to disturb the Day of Dreadful Rest, as we children called it"!

Music - vocal and instrumental - was a popular outlet. In early August 1835 the Belfast Amateur Band performed one of their excursions on a boat along the Lagan, stopping to entertain the appreciative Donegalls at Ormeau; "another Band of Amateurs was also present (that belonging to Mr Kane's glass-house in Ballymacarrett) who continued to play during the intervals ... Both parties deserve the highest credit [for their] proficiency". There were drumming clubs and accordion groups; companies such as Harland & Wolff were to establish their own choirs. With the emergence of the Boys' Brigade, virtually every district of East Belfast was to set up a flute or silver band, and James Galway learned much of his art in the ranks of the 39th Old Boys' Flute Band, originally established in 1917 at Pitt Street Mission on the lower Newtownards Road.

Local pride

The distress faced by East Belfast during the 1920 riots followed hard on the heels of that wrought by the First World War, when so many men went to serve with courage, distinction and sacrifice, primarily in 8th Battalion Royal Irish Rifles. William MacFadzean, who lived in Rubicon (now the surgery of Dr Stephen Rainey and his partners) at the top of the Cregagh Road, won the Victoria Cross for his personal sacrifice on the brutal opening day of the Battle of the Somme (1 July 1916).

Further disruption, scarring and death came with the Second World War, which brought in April and May 1941 the assault of the Luftwaffe upon the shipyards, the Newtownards Road, the Arches, and out towards Stormont. Even the descendants of Victor Coates suffered as their home, Clonallan on the Belmont Road, suffered a direct

People

hit. The fire brigades passed by the blazing home, because they were obliged to give priority to General Hospital no.24 which had also been struck by bombs in the grounds of Campbell College (the pupils had been evacuated to the Northern Counties Hotel in Portrush). By the time the brigade was finished there, Clonallan had been reduced to ashes - perhaps an appropriate symbol of the decline of 150 years of the industrial and commercial greatness of East Belfast.

The district has suffered further tissue damage and scars during the last thirty years of The Troubles, but efforts are currently being made to regenerate the area, and it is hoped that the illustrations in this book will evoke nostalgia for and pride in the area. It is this determination, resilience and pride which has sustained it for five centuries. As Moss & Hume in their history of Harland & Wolff have pointed out: "The expansion of the shipyards had accelerated the growth of East Belfast ... Ballymacarrett became a very self-conscious community,

intensely proud of its achievements and itself ... it contained the biggest ropeworks and the biggest shipyard in the world". Harland & Wolff, it was boasted, was a place where "boys do the work of men, and men do the work of giants", and yet were still sufficiently proud and attentive to finish and polish every rivet as if it were "a walnut sideboard"!

At times, life for many in East Belfast during the last two hundred years must have proved as grim and grey as Con O'Neill's castle. East Belfast has however, for the most part, been sustained and enlivened by the Ulster sense of humour and community spirit. It is hoped that the images of this book revitalise the sense of nostalgia that was echoed a century ago when Gustav Wolff - although he actually lived in a detached residence in Sydenham! - penned the following verse:

You may talk of your Edinburgh and the beauties of Perth,
And all the large cities famed on earth,
But give me my house, though it may be a garret,
In the pleasant surroundings of Ballymacarrett.

90

Bibliography

Bresland, R W, The Backward Glance: C S Lewis and Ireland, (Institute of Irish Studies, Belfast, 1999)

Doherty, J, Standing Room Only: Memoirs of Belfast Cinemas, (Lagan Historical Society, 1997)

Elliott, S M, The World as I Found It, (William Brown, Belfast, 1887)

Hammond, D, Steelchest, Nail in the Boot and the Barking Dog, (Flying Fox Films, Belfast, 1986)

Hill, Rev George (ed), The Montgomery Manuscripts (1603-1706) ... by William Montgomery of Rsosemount, (Archer & Sons, Belfast, 1869)

Jones, E, A Social Geography of Belfast, (Oxford UP, Oxford, 1960)

Lowry, T K, The Hamilton Manuscripts, (Archer & Sons, Belfast, 1867)

McKay, P, A Dictionary of Ulster Place-Names, (Institute of Irish Studies, Belfast, 1999)

Proudfoot, L (ed), Down: History and Society, (Geography Publications, Dublin, 1992)

Redmond, Rev J, Church, State, Industry 1827-1929 in East Belfast, (Belfast, 1929)

Rudnitsky, H, The Careys, (Blackstaff Press, Belfast, 1978)

and numerous, invaluable articles from the volumes of the East Belfast Historical Society Journal, and the many unsung histories of local churches.

Acknowledgements

I am particularly indebted to all my fellow members of the East Belfast Historical Society who have done such valuable research over the last 30 years, especially John Auld, George Doyle, William Hutton, Victor Kelly, Norman Kennedy, William Kirkpatrick, Aileen L'Amie, Charlie Ludlow, Jim Patton, George Platt, Ruby Purdy, Thompie Steele and Wesley Thompson. Thanks are also due to Martin Cooke, Addy Morrow, Campbell College, and the historians, clergy and and officials of the following churches: Belmont Presbyterian, Castlereagh Presbyterian, Knock Methodist, Knock Presbyterian, Mountpottinger Methodist Church, St Finnian's Church of Ireland, St Mark's Church of Ireland and Willowfield Church of Ireland. Much information could not have been obtained without the services of The Public Record Office of Northern Ireland; the Central Library & Newspaper Library in Belfast; and the Linen Hall Library.
- Keith Haines

When I was asked to illustrate this book I was delighted to be given the oportunity and agreed with enthusiasm. The task proved a challenging one and I would like to thank Linda, Pat, Des, Ros, Rosaleen, George, Valerie, Gladys, Thompie, Raymond and Sandra for their support and encouragement.
- Martin Cooke

Dear Reader

This book is from our much complimented illustrated book series which includes:-

Strangford Shores	Donegal Highlands
Dundalk & North Louth	Drogheda & the Boyne Valley
Armagh	The Mournes
Belfast	Fermanagh
Antrim, town & country	Omagh
Inishowen	South Donegal
Heart of Down	Galway
South Armagh	Cookstown
Blanchardstown, Castleknock and the Park	

For the more athletically minded our illustrated walking book series includes:-

Bernard Davey's Mourne   Tony McAuley's Glens
Bernard Davey's Mourne Part 2

Also available in our 'Illustrated History & Companion' Range are:-

City of Derry   Holywood   Ballymoney
Lisburn   Banbridge

And from our Music series:-

Colum Sands, Between the Earth and the Sky

We can also supply prints, individually signed by the artist, of the paintings featured in the above titles as well as many other areas of Ireland.

For details on these superb publications and to view samples of the paintings they contain, you can visit our web site at **www.cottage-publications.com** or alternatively you can contact us as follows:-

Telephone: +44 (028) 9188 8033   Fax: +44 (028) 9188 8063

Cottage

Publications

Cottage Publications
15 Ballyhay Road
Donaghadee, Co. Down
N. Ireland, BT21 0NG